DON'T-KNOW MIND

DON'T-KNOW MIND

The Spirit of Korean Zen

Richard Shrobe

Shambhala

BOSTON & LONDON

2004

Shambhala Publications, Inc.
Horticultural Hall
300 Massachusetts Avenue
Boston, Massachusetts 02115
www.shambhala.com

9 8 7 6 5 4 3 2 1

First Edition
Printed in the United States of America

❀ This edition is printed on acid-free paper that meets the
American National Standards Institute z39.48 Standard.
Distributed in the United States by Random House, Inc.,
and in Canada by Random House of Canada Ltd

Library of Congress Cataloging-in-Publication Data
Wu, Kwang.
Don't-know mind: the spirit of Korean Zen/
Richard Shrobe.—1st ed.
p. cm.
ISBN 1-59030-110-2 (pbk.: alk. paper)
1. Zen Buddhism—Korea—History.
I. Title: Spirit of Korean Zen. II. Title.
BQ9262.9.K7 w8 2004
294.3'927'09519—dc22
2003027040

To my Teacher
Seung Sahn Dae Soen Sa Nim
and to the memory of
Zen Master Su Bong and
Susan Kimberly Shrobe

CONTENTS

DON'T-KNOW MIND

INTRODUCTION

When Zen masters of old noticed embellishments, they would sometimes criticize them as "painting feet on a snake" or as "making waves where there is no wind." Obviously the snake is already complete without our adding feet or legs, and it moves through the world quite adequately according to its own nature; similarly, waves are unlikely where there is no wind.

It is worth noting here that making waves where there is no wind has actually been used to describe the verbal expositions of Zen teachers. Since this book is a compilation of such expositions, the use of this statement demands a bit of explanation.

According to traditional Zen teaching, all of us are already complete and in full possession of true nature. Seen from this most fundamental and radical point of view, we are already enlightened, already Buddha. That being so, it follows that all practices, theories, and techniques become subsidiary. With this in mind, a student once asked a Zen master, "If everything is already clear and complete, why do you open your mouth to give verbal teaching?"

The teacher responded, "Only for you!" In those three words he told why Zen masters teach, knowing that what each listener does with the teachings and practices of Zen determines whether those teachings increase the height of the waves or return the student to his or her original clarity.

Because I aspire to be of some help to students and to fulfill an obligation to my teacher and the teachers of the past, I give Zen talks at Chogye International Zen Center of New York. The material in this book is derived from these talks. Each talk begins with a dynamic presentation characteristic of the Korean Zen tradition. The teacher holds up the Zen stick for all to see, then hits the floor or lectern with it and presents a challenge to the listeners in order to raise the mind of questioning or inquiry. This is typically repeated three times, followed by the traditional Zen shout "KATZ!" that clears all that has preceded it. Immediately, a point of clarity is offered that resolves the initial challenge. Then the body of the talk proceeds. We have, in this book, attempted to transmute this style of opening into a short prologue, poem, or pointer.

The setting for these talks was no serene mountain temple away from the "dusts of the world." Chogye International Zen Center is located in an apartment building on a busy street in Manhattan. The Zen Center is on the second floor, meaning that peaceful practice may be challenged by a wide array of sounds from the street. These teachings were punctuated by fire-engine sirens, traffic noises, and the occasional lilt of rap music from a boom box passing down the block. The teachings themselves also are a mix: a synthesis of the traditional and the contemporary.

Each chapter focuses on the teachings of well-known Zen

masters in the Korean tradition. Korean Zen's history reaches back to eighth-century China and the Sixth Patriarch, Hui-neng (Jap., E'no). A few generations after the death of the Sixth Patriarch, Zen teaching separated into five teaching streams or "schools." Of these five, two have continued into the present: the Rinzai (Chin., Lin-chi-tsung) and the Soto (Chin., Ts'ao-tung-tsung). Korean Zen, however, traces its roots directly back to the Zen of the Sixth Patriarch and his successors. Its origins are therefore seen as being prior to the five-school period. Although the essence, or "bone," of the different streams and traditions are the same, they have different styles of presentation and different techniques. According to the Korean Zen tradition, Rinzai Zen emphasizes Kwan Hwa, or "perceive *kong-an*," which refers to illumination through looking into words; Soto Zen emphasizes Muk Jo, or "perceive silence," in which one just sits and "hits" the world of opposites; and Chogye Zen (the Korean tradition) emphasizes Shi Shim Ma, or "What is this?" which refers to perceiving not-knowing. If you perceive don't-know, just this, itself, is enlightenment. The great modern-day Korean Zen master Ko Bong used to teach, "If you attain don't-know, that is your original master."

A major theme that runs through these presentations is the adequacy or "enough-ness" of the mind before conceptualization, opinion, and ideation; in its universal aspect, not-knowing and not understanding contain a vast array of possibilities. As trust and confidence in this is attained, intimacy and compassion become actualized, and don't-know begins to bestow the gifts of clarity, respect, kindness, and responsiveness. Therefore, the "last word of Zen" involves connecting with all of life and the environment through enlightened, compassionate activity.

Korean Zen masters sometimes exhort and cajole their students with the directive, "Drink cold water." Chinese Zen Master Joju (Chin., Chao-chou or Zhaozhou; Jap., Joshu) used a similar tactic when he responded, "Go drink tea." These teaching instructions simultaneously reveal a number of nuances and meanings. "Drink cold water" sometimes means "Wake up!" It is often intended to point the student toward the actuality of this moment, encouraging him or her to just act clearly. At other times it points the student toward perceiving his or her original mind or true self before thought and conception. For example, here is a comment by Korean Zen Master Seung Sahn:

> Socrates used to walk through the streets and markets of Athens, telling people as he passed, "You must understand your true self, you must understand your true self." One of his students asked him, "Teacher, do you understand your true self?" "I don't know," he replied, "but I understand this don't know." [Zen masters'] and Socrates' actions, are they the same or different? If you attain that, then you attain your true self. If you don't understand, go to the kitchen and drink cold water.[1]

And again, Seung Sahn comments:

> The sky never says, "I am the sky." The tree never says, "I am tree." The dog only barks, "Woof, woof." If you open your mouth, you get thirty blows; if you close your mouth, then you also get thirty blows. What can you do? Put it all down. If you are thirsty, go drink some cold water.[2]

I hope that the material in this book will be helpful to readers in both their formal spiritual practices and everyday life, and that the teachings of the great Korean Zen masters awaken you like the cold, clear water of autumn.

Whenever possible, in addition to using the Korean names

used by the Kwan Um School of Zen, I have given the Chinese and Japanese names as they appear in *The Shambhala Dictionary of Buddhism and Zen* (Shambhala: Boston, 1991).

I wish to thank my teacher Seung Sahn Dae Soen Sa Nim for his clarity and great determination, which continue to be a beacon for me and countless others.

I am appreciative of the efforts of my editors Elizabeth McGuinness and John Holland to retain the free, lively conversational style, while making the material flow in readable form. I would also like to thank Mary Ekwall, Sonya Lazarevich, Daniel Michael, and Jeff Timmins, who painstakingly transcribed the original material. In addition, thanks to Dave O'Neal, Managing Editor of Shambhala Publications and to Susan Briddle, who did the final copyediting.

ORIGINS   *Ma-tsu, Chih-tsang of His-t'ang, and the Early Korean Masters*

MA-TSU'S FOUR WORDS AND ONE HUNDRED NEGATIONS

Can this matter of Zen be explained or not?
Can this matter of Zen be understood or not?
If you say that it can be explained and understood,
*   then you are attaching to words and concepts and*
*   miss the basic fact. On the other hand, if you*
*   say it cannot be understood, then how can the*
Zen Dharma be taught to all beings?
What can you do?
Look clearly!
A crow's head is black.
A crane's head is white.

A *kong-an* (Jap., *koan*) is a phrase from a Buddhist scripture or an episode from the life of an ancient Zen master that points to the nature of ultimate reality. Paradoxical in nature, kong-ans cannot be comprehended by the rational mind and require that one make a leap beyond conceptual thought to another level of understanding. "Four Words and One Hundred Negations" is an old Zen story and kong-an that appears both in *The Blue Cliff Record* and *The Book of Serenity* (two important collections of kong-ans accompanied by commentaries). This is how it goes:

> A monk asked Great Master Ma, "Please, Master, going beyond the 'four words and one hundred negations,' directly point out to me the meaning of the coming from the West." Master Ma said, "I'm tired today and can't explain to you. Go ask Chih-tsang." When the monk asked Chih-tsang, Chih-tsang said, "Why didn't you ask the Master?" The monk replied, "The Master had me come ask you." Tsang told him, "I have a headache today. I can't explain to you. Go ask Elder Brother Hai." So the monk then asked Elder Brother Hai (also known as Pai-chang). Hai said, "At this point, all the more I don't understand." When the monk related this to Great Master Ma, Master Ma said, "Tsang's head is white, Hai's head is black."[1]

Before examining the case (kong-ans are often referred to as "cases" because the term originally referred to legal cases that constituted precedents), I want to say a little about the cast of characters. The three monks named here have a strong connection not only to the Chinese Zen tradition, but also to the Korean Zen tradition. Of these three, a lot has been written about Great Master Ma, whose full name is Ma-tsu Tao-i (Jap., Baso Doitsu; Kor., Ma Jo). There is also a fair amount about Zen Master Pai-chang (Jap., Hyakujo; Kor., Baek Jang). But there is little written about Chih-tsang of His-t'ang (Jap., Jizo; Kor., Ji Jang).

Chih-tsang, who was born in 735 CE, became a novice monk and began following a teacher when he was eight years old. When he was twenty-five, he took full monk's precepts. Later, hearing about the Zen teaching that Great Master Ma-tsu was giving in the mountains, Chih-tsang went to be his student and eventually became his successor.

Ma-tsu was well known and had hundreds of students, but only 139 earned his permission to teach and start Zen groups in different parts of China. Among those 139, Chih-tsang, Pai-chang, and Nan-ch'uan (Jap., Nansen; Kor., Nam Cheon) were considered the greatest. When Ma-tsu died, the monks in his assembly asked Chih-tsang to teach in Ma-tsu's place. He taught for many years before passing away in 814.

A few other stories about Chih-tsang have survived. One tells of the time Ma-tsu sent him to take a letter to the national teacher at the capital. When Chih-tsang got there, the national teacher asked him, "What kind of teaching is Ma-tsu giving these days?"

Chih-tsang, without opening his mouth, walked from the east side of the hall to the west side, then stood still.

The national teacher asked, "Only that? Or is there something else besides?"

Chih-tsang then walked from the west side of the hall back to the east and again stood still.

The national teacher then said, "That's what you have learned from Ma-tsu, but what do you have that's your own?"

Chih-tsang replied, "I've already shown you, Master."

Chih-tsang makes *his* statement when he walks from east to west, west to east, and then stands still. When the national teacher says, "*That* is your teacher's, but what is *yours*?" Chih-tsang replies, "I've already shown you." Zen is not necessarily about developing some kind of originality. Zen is about digesting and assimilating clear perception and clear understanding. If originality emerges, then originality emerges.

When Chih-tsang first left Ma-tsu's temple, he established his own teaching center. Once a layman came for an interview and asked Chih-tsang, "Is there heaven and hell?"

Chih-tsang answered, "Yes, there is."

The layman then asked, "Do the three jewels of Buddha, Dharma, and Sangha exist?"

"Yes, they do."

The layman asked many more questions of a philosophical nature, and with each one, Chih-tsang answered in the affirmative. Finally the layman asked, "Don't you make a mistake by answering this way?"

Chih-tsang replied, "Have you called on other teachers before?" The layman said he had called on Zen Master Ching-shan. "What did Ching-shan have to say?" Chih-tsang asked.

"Ching-shan said that none of these things exist."

Chih-tsang then inquired, "Do you have a wife?" The layman said he did. "Does Zen Master Ching-shan have a wife?"

"No, he doesn't." Then Chih-tsang commented, "Well, for him it's appropriate to say none of these things exist." The layman bowed, thanked him for his teaching, then left.

Around this time, the late 700s to early 800s—long before Zen went into Japan or any of the countries of Southeast Asia— monks came to China from Korea and studied with a number of Great Master Ma-tsu's students. After returning to Korea, they founded what became known as the Nine Mountains Schools, the earliest Zen tradition in Korea. The schools were not different in their teaching, but were located on nine different mountains. Three of the founding masters were students of Chih-tsang, including Zen Master Toui, who died in 825. He had gone to China in 784 and returned to Korea in 818. Actually, both Chih-tsang and Pai-chang recognized his ability and sanctioned him as a teacher.

Not much of Toui's teaching has come down to us. In one

portion that has been preserved, Toui was asked by a scholar about certain philosophical points in Buddhism. In response, he just held up one fist and said, "All of the teachings of the scriptures are contained in this."

The questioner asked, "Then what is the purpose of believing, understanding, practicing, and realizing, and what can these achieve?"

Toui responded:

> Zen is to make one believe, practice, and realize the principle of without thought, without cultivation. What matters is the direct pointing to the true nature of your mind. Therefore, in the five divisions of the teachings there is also, besides the scriptural teachings, mind-to-mind transmission. Worshipping Buddha statues is nothing more than resorting to an expedient for those who do not understand true nature. However many scriptures you have finished reading over the many years, I think you will not understand through them the way of mind-to-mind transmission.

Zen Master Hyech'oi was another who went to China and studied with Chih-tsang, although he arrived in 814, the year Chih-tsang passed away. It is said, however, that Hyech'oi's practice was so strong that Chih-tsang was able to give him sanction and establish him as a teacher even though their contact was short.

According to a story telling of Hyech'oi's arrival in China, he happened to be traveling on a boat carrying a bunch of criminals. When they docked at the port in China, Hyech'oi was mistaken for one of the prisoners and brought before the magistrate. All he would say in his defense was that he was a monk. The magistrate did not believe him and sentenced him along

with the others. After that, Hyech'oi just sat in a deep state of
meditation. He did not protest; he just sat there. The magistrate
decided to execute thirty of the convicts as an example to everyone else, and Hyech'oi was included in that group. As he
awaited execution, Hyech'oi remained in the deep state of meditation. The magistrate thought this was rather odd and asked
who he was. Finally, becoming convinced that Hyech'oi was,
indeed, a monk, the magistrate released him. It is said in the
story that when he was arrested, Hyech'oi did not particularly
protest or look disturbed, and when he was released, he did not
particularly seem overjoyed, he just went on his way.

A short piece of Hyech'oi's teaching also has come down to
us. Hyech'oi said:

> Originally there is no such thing as Buddha, but by neces-
> sity the name was given to him. Originally there is no such
> thing as mind. To attain enlightenment is to realize the
> one thing. For the sake of illustration, it is said that the
> one thing is empty, but it is not really empty—mind of no
> mind is the true mind, wisdom of no wisdom is the true
> wisdom.

Hong-jik, another monk who studied with Chih-tsang, returned to Korea and became a great Zen master. Although little
is known of him, he is mentioned in an inscription on another
Zen master's memorial plaque. It states, "As for Hong-jik's Zen
spirit, he practiced it without any trace of practice, attained enlightenment without any enlightenment. In his daily meditation
he was always quiet like a great mountain, and when he moved
it was as if all the echoes of the great mountain were roaring."

Now, returning to the case, the first paragraph says, "A monk
asked Great Master Ma, 'Please, Master, going beyond the "four
words and one hundred negations," directly point out to me

the meaning of the coming from the West.'" There is a note at the bottom of the page regarding the four words and one hundred negations: "Four words are 'Existence is emptiness, no-existence is no-emptiness.'" These four words are repeatedly negated according to some procedure of Indian philosophy to make one hundred negations. This is in accordance with the philosophy of the *Heart Sutra*. Sometimes the four words are expressed as four propositions: existence, nonexistence, both existence and nonexistence, and neither existence nor nonexistence.

An old commentary says, "Existence is slander by exaggeration. Nonexistence is slander by underestimation. Both existence and nonexistence are slander by contradiction. Neither existence nor nonexistence is slander by intellectual fabrication." Another way of saying that is, "Everything is not it, nothing is not it." This means it is just like the Zen circle: full, empty, complete. Each and every thing is full and empty and complete just as it is.

This case talks about going beyond, or abandoning, the four propositions and one hundred negations, and then asks about the meaning of Bodhidharma's coming from the West. Bodhidharma (Chin., P'u-t'i-ta-mo; Jap., Daruma) was the first patriarch who brought Zen from India to China. "Why did Bodhidharma come to China from India?" is a standard Zen question that means, "What is the living meaning of Buddhism? What is the living meaning of Zen?" You could ask, "Abandoning or not abandoning, going beyond or not going beyond, where is the living meaning of Buddhism not already clear?"

In a later, similar story, Zen Master Ang Sahn (Chin., Yang-shan; Jap., Kyozan) has a dream in which he gives a dharma speech in one of the celestial realms. He mounts the rostrum and hits the gavel on the table, then says, "The Dharma of the great wide vehicle goes beyond the four propositions and the one hundred negations. Listen carefully, listen carefully."

If you listen full of care and allow the true spirit of listening to emerge spontaneously, that is the great, wide vehicle of compassionate connection with this world. To *just listen* is a rare, rare event, but it is nothing special.

In the case, Ma-tsu says it a little differently. He does not say, "Listen carefully, listen carefully." When the monk asks, "Going beyond the four propositions and the one hundred negations (the totality of Buddhist philosophy, everything that is taught in the scriptures and in the teaching), directly point out for me the meaning of the coming from the West (the living spirit of Zen)," he is asking Ma-tsu to show it to him as a living fact, not as verbal philosophizing and conceptualizing. When Ma-tsu says, *"I'm tired today* and *can't explain* to you," those words already reveal the living meaning of Buddhism. No doubt this monk thought Ma-tsu's answer was going to be something extraordinary, something unusual.

In the introduction to this case, written three to four hundred years after the interchange actually happened, there is a statement about this *not explaining*:

> Zen Master Yuan-Wu said, "In explaining the dharma, there is neither explanation nor teaching. In listening to the dharma, there is neither hearing nor attainment. Since explanation neither explains nor teaches, how can it compare to not explaining? Since listening neither hears nor attains, how can it compare to not listening? Still, no explaining and no listening still amount to something."

One of Ma-tsu's other students, Layman Pang, said, "My great attainment is when I'm tired, I sleep; when I'm hungry, I eat." You could add to that a third: "If someone else is hungry, then give them something to eat."

Ma-tsu's teaching, as well as the teaching of his school and his successors, was fundamentally about the function of our natural being—to not hold anything and to just let the function of our natural being emerge: eating time, just eat; sleeping time, just sleep. "I'm tired today" is just *I'm tired today*. That is all. Sad time, just sad. Happy time, just happy. Relating time, just connect. This means, just let your natural function come forward and connect with the situation. That is the impetus for feeding someone else if he or she is hungry. To function naturally does not mean, "I do exactly what I please." It means I let my natural function emerge as it connects with the exact situation I am in. If someone is hungry, connect with that. If someone is sad, connect with that. If someone is happy, connect with that. Moment by moment let the natural function emerge and connect.

Ma-tsu says, "I'm tired today and can't explain to you. Go ask Chih-tsang." If this monk had been really sharp at that time, he would have just bowed to Ma-tsu and said, "It's already appeared, no need to go ask Chih-tsang. Thank you for your not explaining." But the monk did not quite get it, so he innocently went on to Chih-tsang. From one point of view, this story is about three thieves and an innocent. Each of the thieves is teaching something, but the innocent is also teaching something just by his guilelessness.

When the monk asks Chih-tsang, he responds, "Why didn't you ask the Master?"

"But I did ask the Master," says the monk, "and he told me to come here and ask you."

Chih-tsang immediately replies, "I have a headache today and can't explain." *I have a headache* is just "I have a headache," explaining is extra. Chih-tsang's answer is the second revelation of the living meaning of the Zen tradition. Then Chih-tsang tells the monk, "Go ask Elder Brother Hai," and when he does, Hai says, "At this point, all the more I don't understand."

Now we have *can't explain, can't explain, don't understand.* Explaining is the four propositions and the one hundred negations. Not explaining, not understanding, is the transcendence of ideas, concepts, words, and speech. When the monk related this to Great Master Ma, Ma said, "Tsang's head is white, Hai's head is black." This last statement is enigmatic. In the poem after the case, there is a line that says, "Great Master Lin-chi isn't yet a thief who can steal in broad daylight." This relates to a comment Zen Master Seol Bong (Chin., Hsueh-feng; Jap., Seppo) made when he heard a story of Lin-chi's encounter with a particular monk. Lin-chi (Jap., Rinzai) had suddenly put forward something of a shocking nature to this monk. Seol Bong said, "Lin-chi is very much like a thief who steals in broad daylight." This means he has suddenly taken something away from the monk. But the poem says he is not yet a thief who can steal in broad daylight, meaning that compared to the three thieves in this story, Lin-chi is not so sharp; he is not such a clever thief. Those three can pull it off in broad daylight: "I'm tired, can't explain," "I have a headache, can't explain," "At this point, I don't understand." That is real thievery. By comparison, Lin-chi is too rough, too obvious.

In *The Book of Serenity* there is a comment about this particular line: "This is very much like Hu Bai, the thief who was robbed by trickery by Hu Hai."[2] An old Chinese legend tells of a thief named Hu Bai who was tricked by another thief, Hu Hai. One of them wore a white bandana and the other a black bandana. Here, when Ma-tsu is told about Chih-tsang's comment and Pai-chang's (Hai's) comment, he says, "Tsang's head is white, Hai's head is black." This means these two were great thieves, and of those two, the one who had the best trickery was the one who said, "I do not understand."

That is very much at the heart of the Korean Zen tradition: *don't understand, don't know.* If you completely don't-know, then conceptualization is all taken away. This points to the teacher and the teaching as thieves, meaning that the teaching has to have the ability to cut off the flow of words and speech, ideas and concepts, and take that away from the student. If you sit in meditation or observe your mind in daily activities, you may notice that once you get past the stage of settling your distracted mind, you will almost continuously be explaining your experience to yourself moment by moment by moment. We all tend to engage in this ongoing commentary on living, trying to consolidate our ground or to feel more secure about our experience. Yet, this ongoing explanation is, in its fundamental form, a lie. These explanations are not the actual facts of our experience. That is why Ma-tsu and his student Chih-tsang both say, "Can't explain." When the teaching takes away from you, either suddenly or gradually, this ongoing commentary on your own experiences, then you fall into your actual living experience completely, without separation. It is important to have all that commentary stolen away from you. That is why a commentator says that these three are thieves, the third being the greatest thief. If you completely let go of concepts and completely and only don't-know, moment by moment, then each thing becomes clear as it is.

Zen Master Wu-tsu (Jap., Goso), commenting on the line about the head of one thief being white and the other black, says simply, "Mister Dust Sweeper." In Buddhism, you find the word *dust* used in a particular way. For example, there is the story about the Sixth Patriarch's poem. The head monk had written a poem on the wall of the monastery, which said:

> The body is the Bodhi tree [the place where Buddha sat
>   and attained his enlightenment],
> The mind is the clear mirror's stand.
> Constantly we should clean them, so that no dust collects.

Then the Sixth Patriarch composed a poem challenging that one, saying:

> Bodhi [Sanskrit for wisdom] has no tree.
> The clear mirror has no stand.
> Originally nothing.
> Where is dust?"

One time Zen Master Joju (Chin., Chao-chou; Jap,. Joshu) was sweeping the courtyard in his monastery. A monk said to him, "In this immaculate and pristine place, where can you find dust?"

Joju immediately replied, "Here's another little bit," meaning that if you make too much of a big deal about there being nothing, then that is also dust. On the one hand, clean dust; on the other, where is dust?

Dust in Buddhist philosophy means each phenomenal occurrence. For example, if you look at a beam of light indoors, you may see dust particles floating, millions upon millions of phenomena. The whole world of phenomenal experience is referred to as dust because each and every phenomenon is a momentary flash of existence. If you sit in meditation and watch your experience, you will see each thing flash into existence moment by moment by moment.

Sometimes all the various senses are referred to as dust. What this means is, if you relate to seeing or hearing or sensing and feeling in a dualistic way—subject is here, object is over there—that is creating dust. But if subject and object, inside and outside, all—*ptchh!*—come together, then that is complete seeing, complete hearing, complete sensing. Sometimes the whole world is referred to as a "dust world." (Cf. Luke 6:39–42, Eccles. 12:7.)

So in commenting on these thieves by saying, "Mister Dust Sweeper," Zen Master Wu-tsu is implying that we have to sweep away the sense of expectation in our practice. We all come to practice with some set of expectations, some of them quite obvious, some subtle. The longer you practice, the more you see the infinity of expectations we all have the capacity to bring to something as simple as just sitting, just walking, just listening, just eating, just sleeping, just helping someone. It is necessary to sweep away all of those expectations and all of the conceptual superstructure that we build around our experiences. If you do that, then you fall into the world of *just now*, just *as it is*.

I hope that we all can allow the teaching to steal all of that away from us and go on to help this world with its very large headache.

THE
CLASSICAL
PERIOD

*The Teaching
of Zen Master
T'aego*

MEDITATION IN ACTION

What school of Zen is that?
What practice of Zen is that?
What action of Zen is that?
Look! The Zen teacher's staff is brown,
The Buddha who sits on the altar is gold.

T'aego was a great Zen master who lived in Korea around 1300. His writings make a point about practice and about how to recognize your path—a point that I think we need to look into over and over again.

First, however, some background. Throughout the history of the Korean Zen tradition you find two types of figures or teachers. One had some formal connection with the Zen lineage in China. But others were indigenous figures who never had any formal connection with Chinese Buddhism or Chinese Zen lineages. One of these was Won Hyo, who lived around 600, much earlier than T'aego.

Won Hyo had actually started the journey to China. But on his way there, he stopped for the night in some desert region, perhaps in Manchuria, and made camp in a cave. In the middle of the night he woke up and was thirsty, so he walked around seeking something to drink. Eventually he found what seemed to be a cup full of water, drank until he was satisfied, then went back to sleep. The next morning he woke up and saw that the cup was actually a human skull. There was some liquid and other stuff, maybe blood or bits of flesh, still in it. As he saw this, Won Hyo got nauseous and vomited.

In that act of vomiting, he had a profound insight: "Last night I thought this was water and quenched my thirst. This morning I see that it is something else, so I am relating to it quite differently and am sick to my stomach. Therefore, mind makes everything, and without mind everything is empty." With this great insight, Won Hyo decided there was no need to go on to China. He turned back and spent the rest of his life in Korea.

Won Hyo is greatly revered by the Zen sect in Korea, as well as by the *sutra*, or scriptural, sects in Korea, and by the *mantra* and Pure Land sects. All sects in Korea have great respect for him because what he learned and taught relates to all their practices in one way or another.

A century or so later—probably two generations after the Sixth Patriarch—many Korean monks went to China to study Zen and in the process earned certification to be teachers. After returning to Korea, they founded the Nine Mountains Schools of Zen. The temples of these sects, situated on nine different mountains, had a direct, historical, formal connection with Chinese Zen.

Around 1100 Chinul appeared in Korea. Chinul was another revered Zen master who never went to China; his biography does not even suggest that he received sanction to teach from one of the Zen masters in the Nine Mountains Schools lineage. But he apparently had several enlightenments on his own, then began to teach and became greatly revered. His writings are still much respected today.

T'aego was born around 1300, when the Mongols ruled

China, Korea, and most of East Asia. When T'aego was a teen-ager, he had his head shaved and became a monk. In his late teens and twenties he traveled to various Zen centers in Korea. He probably sat the ninety-day winter and summer retreats, and had interviews with various teachers. Toward the end of this period, he began working with a kong-an:

> The ten thousand things all return to one.
> To what though does the one return?

After years of focusing his mind on this question, he had an awakening and wrote an enlightenment poem:

> I swallowed up all the Buddhas and the Patriarchs
> Without ever using my mouth.

According to his biography, he had another deep awakening several years after that, while practicing with the kong-an "*Mu*":

> A monk asked Zen Master Joju, "Does a dog have Buddha nature?"
> Joju said, "*mu*," (which literally means *no*).

T'aego established a Zen center on a mountain close to present-day Seoul. Many students came to him. By this time the Nine Mountains Schools were feuding among each other and had fallen into a kind of decadent decline. After a few years, T'aego decided to go to China. His biography does not say why. He was already an enlightened person and had students, but suddenly he just put the whole thing away and traveled to China. He studied there briefly with a Zen master in the lineage of Zen Master Lin-chi (Jap., Rinzai), who gave him sanction and transmission. T'aego then traveled on to the capital of China, where he was invited to give dharma talks in the palace. Eventually he returned to Korea, where he lived and taught until he was eighty years old.

During those teaching years he had two main concerns: to unify the Nine Mountains Schools into one Zen school while giving new life to the Zen tradition in Korea, and to offer all Koreans new inspiration to live ethical and moral lives, especially in the face of the Mongolian occupation. Sometimes T'aego taught in remote mountain areas in a traditional Zen way. At other times he was called to the capital, where he was appointed spiritual guide to the royal court and required to teach Buddhism to the king.

Several years ago a book called *A Buddha from Korea: The Zen Teachings of T'aego*, translated with commentary by J. C. Cleary, was published in this country. There are several passages in it that inspire me. Most of these bring up a particular point about practice. One selection is a talk T'aego gave in the palace, directed to the king, probably in front of the court. The others are short letters to lay students.

In the first selection, T'aego sets forth what you might call his point of faith or credo. This is the same point of faith emphasized by many teachers of the Lin-chi lineage. It shows, incidentally, how the Korean Zen lineage offers an integration of an earlier teaching that goes back to the Sixth Patriarch with the later line of Zen Master Lin-chi.

The first selection is called "The Mind Ground"[1]:

> At the behest of the King, T'aego gave a brief outline of the basic principles of Zen: ". . . There is something bright and clear, without falsity, without biases, tranquil and unmoving, possessed of vast consciousness, fundamentally without birth and death and discrimination, without names and forms and words. It engulfs space and covers

all of heaven and earth, all of form and sound, and is equipped to function."

Then he goes on further and says:

This one thing is always with each and every person. Whether you move or not, whenever you encounter circumstances and objects, it is always very obvious and clear, clear everywhere, revealed in everything. It is quietly shining in all activities. As an expedient, it is called Mind. It is also called the Path, and the king of the myriad dharmas, and Buddha. Buddha said that whether walking, sitting or lying down, we are always within it.[2]

So, what is it? T'aego is establishing that on the one hand you can look at this thing as being something which is before name, before form, before speech, before words, never moving, never coming, never going, just universally covering everything. But at the same time, you can find this truth revealed in every activity, in every function, because everything is expressing it just as it is. These are the two sides of the coin.

Then T'aego directs some practical remarks to the king:

Your Majesty must contemplate his own inherent mind. During lulls in the myriad functions of state, Your Majesty should sit upright in the palace, without thinking of good and evil at all, abandoning at once all phenomena of body and mind, just like the golden statue of Buddha. Then the false thinking of birth and destruction is totally obliterated, and the obliterating is obliterated, in an instant the mind-ground is quiet and motionless, with nothing to rest on. Body and mind are suddenly empty: it's like leaning on the void. All that appears here is total clarity and illumination.

> At this moment, you should look carefully at your original
> face before your father and mother were born. As soon as
> it is brought up, you awaken to it: then, like a person
> drinking water, you know yourself whether it is cool or
> warm. It cannot be described or explained to anyone else.
> It's just a luminous awareness covering heaven and earth.[3]

There is an interesting practice point here, when he tells the
king to sit up straight and become like a golden Buddha.
"Then," he says, "the false thinking of birth and destruction is
totally obliterated. And the obliterating is obliterated."

In a way that means, first, cut off all thinking. Second, cut off
the cutting off of all thinking; don't hold onto that, either. Then
everything just becomes open and wide and empty. At that
time, what is your original face before your parents were born?
That's the kong-an.

T'aego continues:

> This is the wonder transmitted from "father" to "son" by
> the buddhas and enlightened teachers since antiquity. You
> must make it your concern: be careful not to neglect it. Be
> like this even when attending to affairs of state and work-
> ing for the renovation of the people. Use this Path also to
> be alert to all events and to encourage all of your ministers
> and common subjects to share together in the uncontrived
> inner truth and enjoy Great Peace. Then the buddhas and
> *nagas* and *devas* are sure to rejoice and extend supernatural
> aid in ruling the country.

The next selection is called "The Original Face" and comprises four parts: the first two relate to practice using a kong-an;
the second two are about using a *mantra* (a sacred syllable or
series of syllables that a practitioner continuously repeats).

The first one is addressed to the degree-holder Ch'oe[4]:

> You ask: "What was my original face before my father and mother were born?" If you can understand completely as soon as it is mentioned, then you're through.

That reminds me of the time Ku Sahn Sunim, a Korean Zen master, came to this country when he was quite old. He and Zen Master Seung Sahn (the founder of our school, whom we often refer to as Dae Soen Sa Nim) gave a talk together, and Dae Soen Sa Nim was talking about don't-know mind. Ku Sahn Sunim said, "When you say 'don't-know,' at that time, you have already hit the nail on the head."

Similarly, T'aego says:

> If you can understand completely as soon as it [original face] is mentioned, then you're through. If not [*he is a little more realistic now*], then you should be continuously mindful [of this question] twenty-four hours a day, without letting your mind ignore it, whatever you are doing. Be like a chicken guarding an egg, like a cat stalking a mouse. If you can keep on like this, within three to seven days you are sure to get some measure of accord [with the inner meaning of the question]. . . . As you discuss the skill in means here, you will think: "My physical body, composed of the four elements, was obviously born from my father and mother. At some unspecified time it is sure to decompose. What then was my original face before my father and mother were born?"
>
> Come to grips with this without falling into oblivion, thousands and thousands of times. [*That is a realistic point of practice: As you work on this, do not be discouraged. Just return to practicing with a sincere mind thousands and thou-*

sands of times.] If you are like this without interruption, then naturally your work will become pure and ripe and your body and mind will be clear and content, like the crisp air of autumn.

That is what T'aego has to say about the original face. The next excerpt, written to a different layman, is called, "Who's Asking?"⁵

Knowing that impermanence is swift, and birth and death is an important matter, you have come specially to ask about the Path. This is indeed the conduct of a real man.

Still: who is the one who recognizes impermanence and birth and death like this? And who is the one who has come specially to ask about the Path? If you can discern truly here, Layman, then, as we say, "The visage is unique and wondrous: the light shines on the ten directions. We have just made an offering: now we return to our kin."

Those last sentences actually make up a four-line poem. T'aego says that if you can truly discern here, it is like the following verse. My comments are between the lines.

The visage is unique and wondrous:
[*What kind of visage is that which is clear and wondrous?*]
The light shines on the ten directions.
[*Where can you find this light?*]
We have just made an offering:
[*Oh? What did you offer?*]
Now we return to our kin.
[*Where is the place of return to family?*]

Then he continues:

> Nevertheless: do not stop your potential and linger in
> thought over these four lines using your conceptual mind
> and inbred biases. If you do, the more you explain, the
> farther away you get. Thus it is better to study the living
> phrase.
>
> Haven't you read [this case]? A monk asked Zhaozhou
> [Kor., Joju], "Does a dog have buddha-nature or not?"
> Zhaozhou said, "No." This "No" is not the *No* of existence
> and nonexistence, nor is it the *No* of real nothingness. But
> tell me, in the end, what truth is it?

T'aego responds to that question in another selection, "Con-
templating No," written to another layman[6]:

> When you arrive here, you must abandon all with your
> whole body, not doing anything, not doing not-doing-any-
> thing. [*T'aego makes the same point here as he did about oblit-
> erating, and obliterating the obliterating. First he says you don't
> do anything, then you don't don't-do-anything.*] Go straight to
> the empty and free and vast, with no pondering what to
> think. The previous thought is already extinct, the follow-
> ing thought does not arise, the present thought is itself
> empty.

When practicing this way you should view whatever is occur-
ring in your mind presently as already empty. If it is already
empty, there is no need to push it away, no need to make anything out of it, already just empty. Do not hold onto the emptiness. T'aego is skillful at taking each thing away; anything he
introduces, he then takes away. So the present thought is, itself,
empty. You do not hold onto emptiness. And you forget that

you are not holding onto emptiness. You do not reify this. For-get it. You escape from not re-reifying, and the escape, too, is not kept. When you reach such a time, there is just a spiritual light that is clearly aware and totally still, appearing as a lofty presence.

That is his teaching on *No* and his teaching style of working with a kong-an.

Now here is an excerpt that shows T'aego's approach to mantra practice. It is called "Outline of Essentials for Reciting the Buddha-name" and is addressed to Layman Nagam[7]:

> *Amitabha Buddha* [Jap. & Kor., Amida] is Sanskrit: In our language it means "Buddha of Infinite Life." The word *buddha* is also Sanskrit: in our language it means "enlight-ened one."
>
> The fact is that the fundamental nature of each and every person contains a great spiritual awareness. It is fun-damentally without birth and death. It extends through ancient and modern, spiritually alive and illuminating, un-defiled, wondrous, sovereign, in peace and bliss. Is this not the Buddha of Infinite Life? [*Here he is making a Zen point out of this: that your original mind is the Buddha of infinite life or infinite light. If you were using the* bodhisattva's *name in-stead of the Buddha's, that would identify your original mind as the dwelling place of the* bodhisattva.] Thus it is said, "To illuminate this mind is called being a buddha. To speak of this mind is called the scriptural teachings." The whole great canon of spiritual teachings spoken by Buddha are expedient means to point out the inherent enlightened na-ture of all people. Although the expedient means are many, in essence they teach of the Pure Land of mind and

the Amitabha of inherent nature. If mind is pure, then the buddha-land is pure. If reality-nature appears, then the buddha-body appears. This is precisely what [the scriptural teachings] mean.

The pure wondrous *dharmakaya* of Amitabha Buddha is everywhere in the mind ground of all sentient beings. Thus it is said: "Mind, buddhas, sentient beings—these three are no different." It is also said: "Mind is buddha, buddha is mind. Outside of the mind there is no buddha. Outside of buddha there is no mind."

At this point, T'aego's message to Layman Nagam has repeated a kong-an based on a story about Zen Master Ma-tsu (Jap., Baso; Kor., Ma Jo), whom we discussed in the last chapter. Ma-tsu was a second-generation successor of the Sixth Patriarch, and many monks of the Korean Nine Mountains Schools studied with his successors. The story goes a little beyond our focus at the moment, but it is a good one, worth telling. It seems that one day Ma-tsu said, "Mind is buddha, buddha is mind." Dae Mai, one of his students, picked up this teaching, had some experience with it, then went to sit Zen on a mountaintop. Sometime later, Ma-tsu sent another student to check on Dae Mai. When the student got there, he asked Dae Mai, "What are you practicing these days?"

Dae Mai replied, "I only keep, 'Mind is buddha, buddha is mind.'"

The student said, "Oh, that's very good. But these days Great Master Ma-tsu's teaching is different from before."

When Dae Mai asked, "What is he teaching these days?" the student said, "These days Ma-tsu is teaching, 'No mind, no Buddha.'"

Dae Mai replied, "That old rascal is making a lot of trouble for everybody. As for me, it's only 'Mind is Buddha, Buddha is mind.' "

When the student went back and told Ma-tsu about Dae Mai (whose name means Great Plum), Mat-su said, "Oh, the plum is ripe now."

Now, let's get back to T'aego's message. He continues:

> If you genuinely recite the buddha-name [*Namu Amita Bul, Namu Amita Bul, Namu Amita Bul,* or *Kwan Seum Bosal, Kwan Seum Bosal, Kwan Seum Bosal*], you are just invoking the Amitabha of your own inherent nature.

There is an important point here: If you are simply invoking the Buddha of your own inherent nature, that is essentially like making a resolution. On New Year's Eve when we chant *Kwan Seum Bosal, Kwan Seum Bosal, Kwan Seum Bosal,* that is like making a New Year's resolution to keep the mind of great compassion. If your resolution is sincere, then it is attained in that moment. The moment you bring up that resolution to hold onto the compassionate name of your own essential mind nature or mind energy, there it is. However, being more realistic, T'aego suggests that twenty-four hours a day, whatever you are doing, you should take the words *Amitabha Buddha* and stick them before your mind's eye (meaning, figuratively, paste them on your nose). Let your mind's eye and the buddha-name become fused into one whole, until this continues undimmed from mind-moment to mind-moment. That means one aspect of this practice is to continuously repeat the mantra over and over again, no matter what you are doing, no matter where you are at any time.

Then T'aego adds a second part to it:

> Sometimes turn back and contemplate closely on an intimate level who the one reciting is.

That is an interesting sentence, ". . . turn back and contemplate closely on an intimate level. . . ." Really become intimate with that question, "Who is repeating this? Who is practicing?" Become intimate with your own inner nature. Then:

> After a long period of work, suddenly in an instant, mind and thoughts are cut off, and Amitabha Buddha's real body will appear before you as a lofty presence. Only then will you be sure about the saying, "The one who has never moved is Buddha."

Here is one more from T'aego about repeating the Buddha name[8]:

> Buddha said: "Beyond thousands of millions of buddha-lands, there is a land called Ultimate Bliss. This land has a buddha called Amitabha. Now he appears teaching the Dharma. . . ." In these words of Buddha there is a profound, intimate, esoteric meaning. Do you recognize it or not, Layman?
>
> Put Amitabha Buddha's name in your mind: be undimmed and mindful of it all the time, moment to moment without a break. Come to grips with it and contemplate it earnestly. When your thoughts and ideas are exhausted, then turn back and observe: who is the one mindful of the buddha-name? Also observe: who is the one who can observe back this way?
>
> Give this close detailed study: come to grips with it on an intimate level.

He keeps making this point: on an intimate level. Become intimate with what you are doing. *Intimate* essentially means to completely become one with your activity. Become close, as close as possible. Then:

> Suddenly this mind is cut off and the Amitabha of inherent
> nature appears before you as a grand presence. Work hard
> on it!

That is his advice.

Now, just one more selection from T'aego, called "How to
Study Zen"[9]:

> The days and months go by like lightning: we should
> value the time. We pass from life to death in the time it
> takes to breathe in and breathe out: it's hard to guarantee
> even a morning and an evening. [*So be serious!*] Whether
> walking, standing, sitting, or lying down, do not waste
> even a moment of time. Become ever braver and bolder.
> Be like our original teacher Shakyamuni, who kept on
> progressing energetically. . . .
>
> Put down your myriad of concerns and wake up. At the
> end of the road it's like an iron wall. False thoughts are all
> extinguished, and extinguishing is wiped away: body and
> mind seem to be resting on the void. In the stillness a light
> reaches everywhere with its brilliance.
>
> The original face: who is it? As soon as it is mentioned,
> the arrow sinks in stone. When the mass of doubt is shat-
> tered amidst all the particulars, one thing covers the sky of
> blue.

Then, a little further on he says:

> Our family style is not remote. When tired we stretch out
> our legs and sleep. When hungry we let our mouths eat.
> In the human realm, what school is this? Blows and shouts
> fall like raindrops.

That is a little of T'aego's teaching. It brings up an important
point that I would like to focus on for a moment: Sometimes

the image of Buddha represents the quality of unmovingness, just as Buddha on the altar never moves.

But the *bodhisattva*, who is usually attending the Buddha, represents enlightened, compassionate action in the world. The brown stick is in my hand. So there are always two aspects: stillness, and movement or activity. Most of our life is spent in activity, so how we practice in activity is important. What *is* meditation in action? If we do not find some skillful way of practicing meditation in action, then coming into the Zen Center or practicing formally, as beneficial as it may be, does not carry over adequately into our life as a whole; the path of our practice does not become our way of life. Coming into the Zen Center becomes, then, just a nice thing to do. That is why this notion of meditation in action is very, *very* important.

At Christmas, my daughter gave me a little calendar that has daily Zen quotes. Every day I pull off one of the pages. The calendar is sitting on my desk at work. The other day I pulled off a page that had a quote from Alan Watts: "Zen does not confuse spirituality with thinking about God while one is peeling potatoes. Zen spirituality is just to peel the potatoes." What does it really mean to just peel the potatoes? And how is just peeling the potatoes a spiritual act? Watts makes two distinctions: "Zen does not confuse spirituality with thinking about God while one is peeling potatoes." This brings up the question, what is meditation in action? Just peeling the potatoes? Or thinking about God?

T'aego suggests that "twenty-four hours a day . . . whatever you are doing," always bring up the big question: "What is my original face before my father and mother were born?" So while peeling the potatoes, you ask yourself, "What is my original face?"

This is a little confusing. Couldn't thinking about God be the equivalent of asking "what is my original face?"? Or, keeping the Buddha name or the boddisattva name as a mantra while peeling potatoes, *"Kwan Seum Bosal, Kwan Seum Bosal, Kwan Seum Bosal"*? What kind of practice *is* meditation in action?

Twenty or more years ago, my dharma brother Zen Master Ji Bong (Bob Moore) was fairly new to Zen. He was teaching music at Yale University and working on the kong-an, "What Am I? Don't-Know." He wrote a letter to Zen Master Seung Sahn and said: "You say to keep don't-know mind continuously. But when I'm teaching music in the classroom, if I try to keep this 'What am I? Don't-know,' then I can't really focus on what I'm supposed to be teaching. On the other hand, if I completely focus on what I'm teaching and the students, I completely forget about don't-know. So what should I do?"

Dae Soen Sa Nim wrote back: "You don't understand don't-know. You are only attached to the words don't-know. When you are teaching music, just completely teach music. That's don't-know."

Brother David Steindl-Rast, a Benedictine monk, makes a distinction between what he calls meditation *during* action and meditation *in* action. In his book *Gratefulness, the Heart of Prayer*, Brother David says that meditation or prayer is just meditation or prayer, no matter how you are doing it. But, he adds, people sometimes make difficulties for themselves about all this, so it is helpful to think about it in a certain way.

Offering an example, he explains, "My mother knits all kinds of sweaters for her children and grandchildren and for her great-grandchild. And while she is doing so, she likes to pray the rosary. Now, that is contemplation *during* action. . . . We call it 'Living by the Word.'"[10]

As it says in the New Testament, "In the beginning was the Word, and the Word was with God, and the Word was God."

By repeating the rosary or prayer, Brother David's mother is entering into contemplation through the word.

But then, he says, there is also another kind of prayer, which he describes as "love's world of prayer." His mother's knitting with the spirit of wanting to make an offering to those she cares about—even if she is not repeating the rosary at all—by that act of knitting, she is entering the world of (in Catholic terms) God's love, enacting God's love through lovingly knitting the sweaters. This, he says, is "contemplation *in* action." Translating that into our terms, you could say that this simple activity— knitting things for people and giving them—manifests or actualizes the bodhisattva mind of great love and great compassion.

There are many people who are truly contemplative or meditative types, Brother David says. Among meditatives he suggests that there are two kinds of people, depending upon their situations. Some, like monks and nuns, can spend a lot of time in silence and in formalized prayer or meditation. But then there are others, like a school teacher who must take her class of twenty-seven children on a field trip to the zoo. All day long she must attend to these youngsters, keep them from going off this way and that, help them have fun and see animals and learn what they are supposed to learn. Finally, she comes home and says, "All day long I didn't have a moment to pray." But seen from a different perspective, she was doing nothing but meditating all day long. In the simple activity—well, not-so-simple activity—of attending children on a field trip to the zoo, done with caring, love, and attentiveness, she is continuously engaged in the practice of meditation in action.

The problem comes, of course, when someone sees their circumstance in life as if it were a hindrance to practice. Zen Master Seung Sahn had a kong-an that he used to make a point about this. You would come in for an interview and he would ask, "Why do you eat every day?" The idea was, what is your direction, your purpose?

Robert Aitken Roshi, a Zen master in Hawaii, has made a similar point. He said, "If you're clear about your purpose, then whatever you're doing becomes part of your practice." Calling circumstances in your life obstructions or hindrances to practice is just attaching negative labels to the actual circumstances of your life. And in fact, seen differently, they are no different from your arms and your legs; they are just there to be used in some way. So a hindrance is not a hindrance, and an obstacle is not an obstacle. They are just opportunities.

Brother David makes one more point worth looking at— again, using knitting for his example. "For my mother it's a simple activity," he says. "For me, it's not such a simple activity." But, he adds, during a simple activity like that, it is easy and skillful and helpful to keep some formalized practice going: holding onto your kong-an or mantra, whatever your practice is. If you are keyboarding you might be able to do that; the worst that would happen would probably be that you'd misspell a few words. But if you've got twenty-seven kids on a field trip to the zoo, you'd better not get too absorbed in "what is my original face before my parents were born?" That could be disastrous. At that time your only choice is to use your situation to manifest the mind of caring, compassion, and love. It is helpful to discern, of course, different kinds of situations and to be clear about your direction, and then to be able to use these things as practice. Sometimes we envy someone else's situation; that becomes a difficulty.

One day Zen master Un Mun (Chin., Yun-men; Jap., Ummon) mounted the rostrum to give his dharma speech. He said:

All individual entities are essentially without difference, but we should not stretch the duck's legs, nor shorten the crane's, fill in the valleys and level the peaks, and then say that there is no difference.

This statement was taken from an earlier writing, which is almost the same but has another little point connected to it. The original writing says:

To stretch the duck's legs would cause it pain and to cut off the crane's legs would make it suffer; therefore, what is by nature long needs no cutting off, and what is by nature short needs no stretching.

Is it an obstacle? Is it a hindrance? Or is it an opportunity? The choice is entirely up to you. But when you recognize that the path you are on as an individual is a path of no choice, or only one choice, then you recognize that whatever you encounter is not an obstacle or a hindrance; that it is, in fact, the path. At that time your purpose, your direction, and your practice all become one. Whether doing formal practice or trying to hold some practice in your daily life, do not stretch the duck's legs or cut off the crane's, because you only create pain and suffering for yourself. Compassion begins at home, love begins at home, and skillful means also begin at home.

THE WORLD AS SPIRITUAL PRACTICE

> *See color, hear sound.*
> *Is that intimate or not?*
> . . . .
> *Winter's leaving is embraced by spring's approaching.*
> *Aahh!*

In the previous chapter, I offered some teachings of Zen Master T'aego; now I want to present some of his poems. One theme that appeared out of the readings last time had to do with meditation in action, and I want to pick up on that again. In these poems, you will see something about meeting the phenomenal world in a particular way as spiritual practice.

There are six poems, all short, just four lines. The first is:

> *How Can I Speak?*[1]
> All phenomena are beyond names and forms
> The sounds of the streams and the colors of the mountains
>   are closest
> What is "closest"?
> You can only please yourself: how can I speak?

That first line, "All phenomena are beyond names and forms," offers an interesting statement. Usually, when people

think about spirituality and meditative practice, a certain erro-
neous notion arises: We should get to a place of complete silence and stillness, a place apart from and beyond all names and
all forms. But here T'aego says that all phenomena themselves
are already beyond names and forms. Sometimes my teacher
used to say, "The sun never says, 'I am the sun'; the moon
never says, 'I am the moon.' So all phenomena are beyond
names and forms."

The poem's second line says, "The sounds of the streams and
the colors of the mountains are closest." Sometimes you see the
word *closest* used in this kind of poetry. *Closest* has the connotation of intimate connection, of becoming one with. To become
completely *intimate with* is to become *close*. So we might read
that line as, "The sounds of the streams and the colors of the
mountains are most intimate." Closer than the name *stream*, or
the name *mountain*, or the pictures we hold in our minds. Just
hearing the sounds of the stream and seeing the color of the
mountain, that is closest, much more intimate.

One time when Zen Master Un Mun mounted the rostrum
to give his dharma speech, he said, "See color, get enlightenment; hear sound, attain the path." So, hear the sound of the
stream, see the color of the mountain, attain closeness or intimacy.

This is all nice talk, *intimacy, closeness*. But then T'aego
throws in one more line: "What is 'closest'?" This is a kong-an.
What is closest is, in fact, the very not-knowing, the question.
The kong-an is closest. If you use the word *closest*, what is that?
If you talk about intimacy, what is intimacy?

Maybe fifteen or twenty years ago, there was an American
teacher—not a Zen teacher or someone in the Zen lineage. He
came from a Hindu background, but had broken away from
that. He taught his students a meditation that was a kind of

inquiry. Moment by moment and in every experience, you were supposed to ask yourself, "Avoiding relationship?"

What is relationship? What is closest? What is most intimate?

When Zen Master Peop An (Chin., Fa-yen) came to his final teacher, he had been traveling around as an itinerant monk. That was typical of monks in China at that time. They traveled hundreds of miles from one temple to the next on a kind of pilgrimage, calling on different masters to get teaching and to test themselves. This final teacher of Peop An's asked him, "What is the meaning of your travels?" The question surprised Peop An, and he had nothing to say for a minute. Then he said, "Don't know." The teacher replied, "Don't-know is closest to it."

What is *closest*?

The last line of the poem reads: "You can only please yourself: how can I speak?" You have to find it yourself, I have no words to give you about this. Look deeply into it.

The next poem is:

> *One Gate*[2]
> The whole world is one gate:
> Why don't you come in?
> When you have penetrated Zhaozhou's *No* [the
>   fundamental question],
> At last the chains will open by themselves

It begins with a wonderful couplet, "The whole world is one gate: Why don't you come in?" Often we have a subtle, stand-offish attitude. I know that was a deep sickness of mine for many years. Now it is only a little sickness! "The whole world is one gate; why don't you come in?" Why not take a step forward? Like the old Zen saying, "How do you take one step forward off the flag pole a hundred feet high up in the air?"

Experience is always calling, calling, calling, and asking for our response; yet so often we hold back our responsiveness, deadening our lifelines, vitality, and energy that could meet the world head-on and become one fabric with it.

Zen Master Hyang Eom used an extreme image to bring this point home. He said this matter of Zen is like a man up a tree. His hands are tied behind his back; his feet are also tied and bound. He cannot get a grip on the branch, and cannot get a foothold to secure himself. He hangs from the branch by his teeth. As if this were not bad enough, someone under the tree asks, "Why did Bodhidharma come to China?" Bodhidharma brought Zen from India to China, so the question means, "Please give me the essence of the Zen tradition's teaching." If the man keeps his mouth closed, he evades his duty to teach and respond in an alive, vital manner; he is dead up in the tree. If he opens his mouth, he will fall.

Then the kong-an asks, "If you are this person in the tree, how can you stay alive?" That is *our* task. How can we stay alive? So often we tie our hands in some way, bind our feet and then grab hold of one thing as if our entire existence depended on it. In doing so, we cut *off* the free-flowing vitality of existence. It is a sad state of affairs. Yet, reality is shown simply in the poem's opening lines, "The whole world is one gate: Why don't you come in?"

When you have penetrated the fundamental question—What am I? What is true self? What is my existence? What is this?—when you have come to terms with and penetrated that, at last the chains will open by themselves. It is not that at that moment, like a miraculous event, the chains will open. Rather, at that moment you will perceive that the chains were never there in the first place! That it was all a construction.

It is like the story of the Second Patriarch (Chin., Hui-k'o;

Jap., Eka) who persistently asked for Bodhidharma's instruction while standing in the snow outside a cave at Shao-lin Monastery, where Bodhidharma was practicing. When he finally relented, Bodhidharma asked the monk, "What is it that you want?"

The monk said, "My mind is not at peace. Please pacify my mind."

Bodhidharma replied, "Take out your mind and bring it here, and I will pacify it for you."

The monk said, "When I look for my mind I can't find it."

Bodhidharma said, "Then I already pacified your mind."

Already, that is a very important word in our practice tradition. Already we are all Buddha. Already we have attained enlightenment. Already the chains have been thrown off. But we do not see that. We construct and create and invent all kinds of chains and shackles and bindings for ourselves. So just perceive, "The whole world is one gate: Why don't you come in."

The next poem is:

> *Cloudy Mountains*[3]
> White clouds—inside the clouds, layers of green
>   mountains
> Green mountains—in the mountains, many white clouds
> The sun is the constant companion of the cloudy
>   mountains
> When the body is at peace, there's no place that's not
>   home

Reread those first two lines. They are a poetic restating of the *Heart Sutra*'s teaching, "Form is emptiness, emptiness is form." Then, "The sun is the constant companion of the cloudy mountains": The sun is always shining brightly in the sky. Clouds come, clouds go. But there is always one thing that is not moving, not dependent on coming and going. Then T'aego concludes, "When the body is at peace, there's no place that's not home."

When I was in Korea a couple of years ago I bought some calligraphy. One of those selections had been sitting in a box in my apartment ever since. Recently my wife, who works for the New York University Graduate School of Art History, got a new office. She asked if she could have the calligraphy to hang there. We opened the box, looked at the calligraphy, and I told her what it meant. The characters say, *Dae Do Mu Mun*. *Dae Do* means "great way"; *Mu Mun* means "no gate." If you insert an English word, it reads, "The great way has no gate." *Great way* doesn't mean greater than anything else. *Great* here has the connotation of complete. To realize the complete way is to be completely in touch with what is, moment by moment; not to be holding back and living in some imaginary world of shackles, chains, fantasies, yearnings, hopes, longings, regrets, and all the other things we get caught up in. The great way has no gate.

The word *gate* has a dual connotation. A gate, of course, is something that opens and closes. It also has the connotation of a barrier. Sometimes that word is translated as *checkpoint*, like the barrier that exists between one country and another, the place where you show your passport.

The great way has no barrier, no gate. In one sense that means that wherever we are, at that moment—whatever our activity, if we are entering it completely and not getting caught up in separating subject from object and inside from outside— then, at that moment, there is no barrier, no gate. The gate has already been opened. There is no hindrance, no obstacle, only an enlightened way of being and functioning in the world.

My wife hung the calligraphy on her wall and asked the professor who is their leading expert in Asian art to tell her its meaning. Maybe she did not trust my interpretation. He said the meaning was "smooth sailing."

When T'aego says, "When the body is at peace, there's no place that's not home," it is all smooth sailing. You feel at peace and at rest wherever you are.

The next couple of poems move into the realm of emptiness. The first is called:

> No Pattern[4]
> One thing that exhausts form and sound
> Formless and nameless
> The myriad forms of being arise from this
> Material transformations seem like spirit work

"The myriad forms of being arise from this," from this great plenum void. All forms arise from this. "Material transformations seem like spirit work": Right in this material world of changing, changing, changing, if you see that all of these material transformations are coming from and returning to that one thing that is before name and before form, then this very world and its transformations are the work of the spirit.

In Tibetan Buddhism and in Japanese Shingon Buddhism, they use a visual device called a *mandala*. It is a colorful series of concentric circles, decreasing toward a central point. Buddhas, bodhisattvas, gods, and demons—all kinds of things—inhabit the circles. Many different elements and energies are represented by these entities. The meaning of this kind of technical and meditational mandala, which is used in formal practice, is that all phenomena appearing around this central hub are transformations of one central principle. But the *spontaneous* mandala is just what is appearing right here and now. The myriad phenomena, themselves, are the spirit at work. They "seem like spirit work" if you are not separating, if you can experience it.

Now the next poem:

Merging with the Void[5]
Empty but aware, void but wonder-working
Without "knowledge," illumination is complete.
Though among the myriad phenomena, not standing in
relative opposition to them
Responding to their potentials by manifesting an ocean of
meditative states beyond measure

"Empty but aware": That means, when you ask yourself completely, "What am I?" you come to a point where there are no words, no speech—"When I look for *I*, I don't find anything"—empty. But something there *is* clear and aware. "Empty but aware, void": No entity is there. "[B]ut wonder-working": Seeing comes from there, hearing comes from there, tasting comes from there, feeling comes from there, movement comes from there. Everything comes from there. "Without 'knowledge'": Without knowing, not-knowing. "[I]llumination is complete": When you let go of all your ideas, it is already bright and shining, right in front of you.

The third line begins, "Though among the myriad phenomena": Sitting right in this world. "[N]ot standing in relative opposition to them": Not pushing away, not drawing toward, not making opposition. Just being there with everything. Then, "Responding to their potentials by manifesting an ocean of meditative states beyond measure": Responding to the potentials of all phenomena is itself manifesting meditative states beyond measure. That means, if your action is clear, if your action is precise, then that is already meditation.

Meditation in action does not necessarily mean that as you walk down the street you repeat to yourself, *"Om Mani Padme Hum, Om Mani Padme Hum, Om Mani Padme Hum,"* or keep questioning, "Who is the one who is walking now?" Those techniques *can* be useful. However, if you see your action as a manifestation of what *is*, then that already is manifesting a meditative state and there is no need to resort to a particular technique. It is because we *don't* see such a manifestation that we pick up some technique and start practicing to bring ourselves back to point zero. Then just seeing is possible, just hearing is possible. So "responding to their potentials" means to be able to respond to what is potentially right in front of us in this world of need. That is a meditative state; it is the compassionate activity of a meditative mind.

Many years ago, before I came to Zen, I was a yoga student. I studied with Swami Satchidananda at the Integral Yoga Institute. There was a story about Swami Satchidananda's teacher, Swami Sivananda, who lived in Rishikesh, in the Himalayas, where he had an ashram. He was famous throughout India; many people would go there to see him. Artists, musicians, and other talented people would visit and perform in the ashram.

One time a flute player came and said, "Swamiji, I want to play for you."

Swami Sivananda said, "Fine, go ahead and play."

The whole *sangha* (spiritual community) was sitting there. But when this guy took out his flute and began playing, they all realized that he sounded terrible! He couldn't blow his nose, let alone a flute! When he finished, Swami Sivananda said, in all seriousness, "Wonderful! I award you the title of master flutist."

When the man left, the disciples asked the swami, "How could you do that? It will make titles meaningless."

This story has some similarity to the situation of Kwan Um Zen when I first came into this school, soon after Zen Master Seung Sahn came to the United States. It was not long before some of us were given these long robes, with the title of dharma teacher. Now the actual title in Korean, *Peop Sa*, means "dharma master." Yet here we were, some of us new Zen students, maybe practicing only a year or two, already wearing these long robes. In Korea such robes are given only to those who have been practicing for years and years. Somehow, however, we learned to grow into them.

When the flute player returned to Swami Sivananda's ashram the following year, he said, "Swamiji, I want to thank you for giving me the title of master flutist last year, and I want to play for you again."

Swamiji said, "No problem." Of course, when he played this time, his music was beautiful and masterful.

The last line of T'aego's poem is, "Responding to their potentials by manifesting an ocean of meditative states beyond measure." The image of the ocean in Buddhism is that the ocean can receive and embrace everything. Of course, we know today that this is not true; ecologically it is becoming a disaster. But back then, probably the ocean *could* embrace everything, and the line reflected that. From the standpoint of practice, this line again points us toward our primary direction of openness, compassion, and responsiveness.

And now, the last poem:

> *The Path of Emptiness*[6]
> This emptiness is not empty emptiness
> This Path is not a path that can be considered a path
> Where peaceful extinction is totally extinct
> Perfect illumination is complete and final

"This emptiness is not *empty* emptiness. This path is not a path that can be considered a *path*." Then what is it? For me, the last sentence recalls a pair of lines from one of Master Seung Sahn's poems: "After so much suffering in nirvana [*peaceful extinction*] castles, what a joy to fall back into this world."[7] In his book *Zen Mind, Beginner's Mind,* Suzuki Roshi counsels that when you do something, be like a great bonfire that completely burns itself, leaving no trace.[8] All of them are saying, when you do something, anything, just completely do it at that time, without leaving any trace of self. Then you and the action become one. It is an idea that resurfaces in a line from one of W. B. Yeats's poems: "How can we know the dancer from the dance."

There are two ways of looking at this idea. When practicing, for instance, we may try to do each activity completely: When sitting, we try to make the posture very precise; when breathing, we perceive each breath clearly. We try to pay attention in a particular way, cultivating the art of it, so to speak. In doing that kind of precision work, there is sometimes a moment—when you are really focusing and getting into one thing—when all other distractions drop away. That is a moment of real clarity and sharpness. That is one way.

Maybe I can explain the other way best through recounting an experience of one of our Zen Center members, who recently served as head dharma teacher for a three-day retreat. In this role, he kept discipline in the meditation hall and made sure everything ran smoothly, not letting things get too tight or too loose. When giving a talk later, he said that part of the job was to "not try too hard." He said that as long as he was just being aware he could perceive what was arising in the whole room situation, as well as in everyone's individual situation. The need for something would become clear; it would emerge. Then he could perceive that "now it's time to tell people to sit more still," or "now it's time to institute this or that rule." There wasn't a lot of thinking involved, or striving to make anything more perfect.

In a situation such as this, when you are there with presence, you can sense what is needed at any particular time. And that sensing is skillful, coming from a sense of ease. Thus, it leaves no trace of self in the activity. If you are totally at ease, smooth sailing; what appears in front of you is clear. When you are at ease, it looks as if you have a lot of time to do something. Even with something that requires an instantaneous reaction, there is enough space and enough time around it to be responsive. But when you are not at ease, everything is difficult. This is an important point in our practice.

A couple of weeks ago, I received a newsletter from the Providence Zen Center, which included a talk Zen Master Seung Sahn gave in Hong Kong. He told about a woman there who had asked him a question. "My husband wants to open a fish restaurant in China," she had begun, "and he has a good plan. Probably it would be a very successful business. But I began to think that a fish restaurant is a place where many living creatures are killed, and that would be bad karma. I tried to talk him out of it, but my reasons are not compelling enough and I don't think that he will pay any attention to me." Then she had asked the Zen master, "How would you talk him out of it?"[9]

Dae Soen Sa Nim responded by telling her a story. It is one I heard him tell many years ago. I remembered part of it, but not the whole context, so I was glad to see it again.

The story takes place at the time when Shakyamuni Buddha lived in India. It tells of a man whose regular job, his daily job, was killing cows. Every day, a cow would come in front of him, he would hit it on the head with a hammer, and the cow would cry out "Mooo" and die. The man did not like this job, because he was a follower of the Buddhist teaching. But at that time in India, with its caste system, it was not possible to change jobs. In the caste system there were the priests, the Brahmans, who were in the highest class. Then there were the kings and the warriors, then the merchants, and then the people who had the lowest-class jobs, like hitting cows on the head and killing them. This man talked to his parents about this situation. They said, no, it would not be possible for him to change his job. So he kept doing it.

One day Shariputra—one of the Buddha's main disciples, who had completely attained the essence of the sutras that deal with emptiness—came walking by the slaughterhouse. This man said to Shariputra, "The Buddha and the precepts teach non-killing, but I have this job killing cows every day, so I am making a lot of bad karma. What should I do?"

Shariputra asked, "Who kills the cow?"

The man said, "I kill the cow."

Shariputra then asked, "Who are you?"

The man said, "I don't know."

And Shariputra replied, "Only keep this don't-know mind while you kill cows. Then you won't make bad karma."

After that, Shariputra left and the man kept doing his job: Pow! Moooo! Pow! But the question, "Who is killing the cow?" kept growing bigger and bigger. Finally he was so consumed with the question that his guilt transmuted into a feeling of great perplexity, "Who is killing the cow?" One day a cow came in front of him. Pow! Moooo! Pow! When he heard that last Pow! his mind opened and he got enlightenment. At that moment he could perceive, "I am one with the Buddha! There is no birth, no death."

Then Dae Soen Sa Nim had said to the woman who questioned him, "Any job is no problem. But what is your attitude toward the job? Is the job for you? Or for something that extends beyond just you?" Then, being the sly rascal that he is, he added, "So, if you make a lot of money at this restaurant, you can take some of that money and build a Buddhist temple where people can practice. That would be wonderful!"

Now, of course, the story he told about the man and the cow presents a number of problems, because someone can use that kind of approach as a rationalization for almost anything. Yet, there is an important point to the story: It says this person had no choice. According to the social structure of that time, he had to do that job.

The woman who asked about the fish restaurant was in a similar situation: Her choice was to go along with her husband or to get a divorce. We all find ourselves in this kind of situation at times. We can use the situation as an opportunity for mindfulness, for clarity in expressing compassion in some way, or for seeing deeply into something. Or we can choose to use it as an opportunity to grumble and mumble and make ourselves unhappy.

This does not apply, of course, to situations where there really is a choice, although you may rationalize it away. But when there truly is none, if you can see and use that as practice, then every place you are in is your home. And that, incidentally, is the true meaning of becoming a monk or a nun: realizing that the whole world is your home. If you can use the situation of *no choice*—whether you become a monk or a nun in a formal sense, or continue in lay life—the practice then becomes renunciation: letting go of small *I* and opening to the situation. The world opens at that time.

There is one more reflection I want to offer you. A couple of weeks ago I was at the New Haven Zen Center, where I gave a talk and led a weekend retreat. After my talk, one of the long-time students there spoke briefly before I answered questions. At the end of his remarks, he read this piece from Nelson Mandela's inaugural speech in 1994:

> Our deepest fear is not that we are inadequate. Our deepest fear is that we are powerful beyond measure. It is our

light, not our darkness that most frightens us. We ask ourselves, "Who am I to be brilliant, gorgeous, talented and
fabulous?" Actually, who are you *not* to be? You are a child
of God. Your playing small does not serve the world.
There is nothing enlightened about shrinking so that other
people won't feel insecure around you. We are born to
manifest the glory of God that is within us. It is not in just
some of us, it is in everyone. As we let our own light
shine, we unconsciously give permission to other people
to do the same. As we are liberated from our own fear,
our presence automatically liberates others.

That is a wonderful statement of bodhisattva action: something
that looks like pride, but is not egoistic in spirit. I hope we can
all attain that.

MIND REVOLUTION

Truly, what is north and what is south?
Can true being be found somewhere or nowhere?
Irrelevant!
Just now, feet pointing to the ground, head pointing
*   toward the sky.*

Zen Master T'aego dedicated a number of his poems to figures in the Buddhist sutras or the Zen tradition. In a poem about Hui-neng, he wrote:

The Sixth Patriarch[1]
[Hui-neng of Caoqi, "Workman Lu"]
As he happened to hear the *Diamond Sutra*
It switched his eyes around
Because he venerated the Dharma
He did not fear the journey
When he visited Huang Mei, the fifth patriarch was getting
    old
Peach blossoms red, plum blossoms white, willows so
    green
We can sympathize with all the days he spent on the
    treadmill wearing a weight

> But for him, how could there be the least bit of trouble?
> The grain had already been ripe a long time
> In the middle of the night, he entered the fifth patriarch's
>   room
> The fifth patriarch personally passed on to him the
>   Dharma robe
> His life was hanging by a thread
> So he secretly crossed the West River by moonlight
> Who knew at that time?—he was glad to leave

When the Sixth Patriarch was still a young boy, his father—a civil servant in some small town in southern China—died. The family was poor, so the boy helped support his mother and family by gathering firewood in the hills, then selling it in the town.

Beyond his personal history, the Sixth Patriarch's life story tells about the spirit of practice, something relevant to all of us, right here, right now. So we need to see ourselves in him in some way.

Some versions of the story say that while the young boy was walking through town one day, he happened to hear someone chanting the *Diamond Sutra*. Then, standing there captivated, he heard a particular line and had an insight or awakening. T'aego describes that moment in the poem's first two lines, "As he happened to hear the *Diamond Sutra,* it switched his eyes around," meaning that he saw something quite differently.

The Mind-Only School of Buddhist philosophy has a related phrase, *the revolution of consciousness*. Zen Master Seung Sahn sometimes used to say that Zen is a mind revolution. The word *revolution* here does not necessarily suggest a great warlike campaign—the chopping down of enemies of the Dharma. Rather, it connotes something radically revolving and turning around, causing the perspective from which you see things to suddenly shift. It is quite revolutionary to see things in a different way, even though, concretely, nothing has actually changed.

Maybe, taking a more common kind of event, you could compare it to the experience some of us have had searching for our keys. We look all over the place, then all of the sudden we realize the keys were there, on the table in front of us, the whole time. That is a mind revolution, at that moment.

The line of the *Diamond Sutra* that changed the boy's mind, according to the stories, was, "Dwelling nowhere, let the mind come forth." That line, if you think about it, could be used to describe the style of practice emphasized in the Korean Zen tradition. "Dwelling nowhere" means don't-know. Completely don't-know. The primary dwelling place is found, presumably, in the sense of *I*-ness. Yet, when you look into *I* to find your primary dwelling, you suddenly recognize that you don't know *I*: "What is *I*? Don't know." *That* is abiding nowhere. Then, if you don't hold onto anything, your natural mind emerges and you see clearly: Floor is brown, wall is white.

I looked in the *Diamond Sutra* and could not find the exact phrase that T'aego presumably refers to, but I did find a few similar ones. They are interesting and they relate to our practice. In one section, Buddha is talking to a disciple named Subhuti, instructing him about the practice of an enlightened being, one who is trying to manifest enlightened activity in the world. Remember that a primary practice of the bodhisattva is to raise a great vow, a great intention. That is why we start our morning practice by saying the Four Great Vows. The first is, "Sentient beings are numberless; I vow to save them all." That is called *a great intention*.

Here the Buddha makes the same point, saying, "Subhuti, all the bodhisattvas should give rise to a pure and clear intention, in this spirit. When they give rise to this intention, they should not rely on forms, sounds, smells, tastes, tactile objects, or objects of mind. They should give rise to an intention with their minds not dwelling anywhere."

When you say, "Sentient beings are numberless; I vow to save them all," with intention but without dwelling anywhere—meaning that your mind is not dwelling in the idea of sentient beings, or in the idea of yourself, or in the idea of saving anything—that is called *saving all sentient beings*.

Further on, the Buddha says, "Subhuti, when a bodhisattva gives rise to the unequal mind of awakening, he has to give up all ideas. He cannot rely on forms when he gives rise to that mind, nor on sounds, smells, tastes, tactile objects, or objects of mind. He can only give rise to that mind that is not caught up in anything." So don't hold onto anything, don't attach to anything, don't cling to anything, don't fabricate anything, don't make anything. That is called *giving rise to the mind of awakening*.

A little further on, the Buddha brings up the idea of generosity, or giving out something. Generosity is the first of the *paramitas* (meaning great transcendental acts), which are the bodhisattva's primary practices. Buddha says, "A bodhisattva who still depends on *notions* of practicing generosity is like someone walking in the dark. He will not see anything. But when a bodhisattva does not depend on notions of practicing generosity, he is like someone with good eyesight walking under the bright light of the sun. He can see all shapes and all colors." The point is that while practicing generosity, one transcends the *notion* of "I am being generous."

The third and fourth lines of the poem read, "Because he venerated the Dharma, He did not fear the journey." This practice that we are engaged in is not a quick fix. In fact, we may say it does not fix anything. We may have come to this practice because something has caught our attention, hit us in the heart, and given us a kind of aspiration. It may be that we have heard some aspect of teaching that has given us a little mind revolution. Or maybe we have taken a look at our life in some way and seen that the things that appeared to be important do not quite satisfy us. At that point, we have an aspiration for something else. And there a journey begins.

According to the story, when the Sixth Patriarch first heard the lines in the *Diamond Sutra*, he asked the monk, What was this wonderful teaching that he had been chanting, and where did he learn it? The monk said it was the teaching of the *Diamond Sutra*, and that he had learned it from the Fifth Patriarch of Zen in northern China. Hui-neng, the future Sixth Patriarch, decided he would go to the north and seek teaching from the Fifth Patriarch. His mother encouraged him to go, so he found neighbors who agreed to look after her, then made the long, arduous journey of hundreds and hundreds of miles to the north of China.

There are, of course, many kinds of arduous journeys, not all connected with traveling. I heard about one the other day during an interview on National Public Radio. The subject was a man who had been an extremely committed and determined young jazz piano player, practicing eight to ten hours a day, in the late 1940s or early 1950s. Eventually he became singer Mel Torme's accompanist, but that ended abruptly when he developed severe tendonitis from practicing so intensely in an incorrect way. He could not control his hands any longer; he had to have his wrists taped just to keep them in one position. Yet, instead of giving up, he began searching for some new way to play the piano, focusing on other muscles. He eventually devised a method using only the muscles in his forearms and shoulders. But that only allowed him to play two or three minutes at a time; he would have to wait several weeks for his muscles to recuperate before playing again. The rest of the time, he said, he was "playing the piano in my mind."

Along the way, someone managed to hook up a recording device. Every time the pianist played, the device would flip on. Many months later, he recorded a complete CD and is working on a second! During the program, he actually performed for about two minutes. His playing was beautiful. As he finished, the interviewer said, "Now you won't be able to play for another two months!" The pianist replied, "Yes, that's the way it is, but I accept that."

Sometimes our Zen practice is like that, too. We start with a big bang, make a big push, sit a lot of retreats, sit many hours, or are very involved. Then, at a certain point, that begins to break down. We then have to reestablish our vow, our commitment, and our intention in a way that works for us and adjusts to our life circumstances. All of us, also, need to "not fear the journey," even though many roadblocks seem to appear along the way.

The fifth line in the poem reads: "When he visited Huang Mei [the mountain where the Fifth Patriarch had his temple], the Fifth Patriarch was getting old"—meaning he was soon going to die. After the Fifth Patriarch dies, where will we be able to find him? T'aego answers that immediately: "Peach blossoms red, plum blossoms white, willows so green." That is where we can find the Fifth Patriarch even now. Tomorrow when you go out, look for him. The trees are blooming.

When the Sixth Patriarch got to the temple in the north, he went to have an interview with the Fifth Patriarch, who asked, "Where are you coming from and what do you seek here?"

The Sixth Patriarch replied, "I've come from the south of China. I am not seeking anything and want to become Buddha."

Then the Fifth Patriarch tested and challenged him by saying,

"You barbarians from the south have no Buddha nature; how could you possibly become Buddha?"

The Sixth Patriarch quickly responded, "As far as human beings go, there is north and south. But in the Buddha nature there is nothing like that."

The Fifth Patriarch realized there was something unusual in this young man, but did not acknowledge him openly. Instead, he immediately sent him to the rice-pounding shed. In the monasteries of that time, there were the monks who lived there, and usually some lay people who were entertaining the idea of becoming monks. When those people first entered the monastery, they were usually assigned to do work practice. The Sixth Patriarch was sent to the rice-pounding shed and stayed there about eight months, pounding rice.

The seventh line in T'aego's poem says, "We can sympathize with all the days he spent on the treadmill wearing a weight." I have some idea of what that was like because when I was in Korea, I was taken to a place called Korean Folk Village, where a display of antiques showed the way of life in Korea a couple of centuries ago. Among the antiques was something that looked like a small treadmill, attached to a weight. This contraption was connected to a big mortar containing rice. Somehow or other, when you walked on the treadmill, it pounded the rice, loosening the kernels. Such is our life!

We all feel as if we are on a treadmill sometimes. We get up in the morning, dress, eat breakfast, go to work, interact with others, return home, undress, sleep. The next day we do the same thing. It is very ordinary. Once I looked up the word *ordinary* in the dictionary. One meaning is *perpetual*. That means continuously perpetuating something. Continuously appearing and disappearing. You can see that on the treadmill, or in your ordinary life. These experiences form the field of our practice.

T'aego says, "We can sympathize with all the days he spent on the treadmill wearing a weight. But for him, how could there be the least bit of trouble? The grain had already been ripe a long time." Why can we sympathize? Because we also understand that.

When you stop seeing your actual circumstances as a hindrance or impediment or obstacle, then that becomes the field of practice. T'aego asks, How could any of the dreary work on the treadmill have been an obstacle? The grain had already been ripe. Hui-neng had already experienced something.

It is interesting that even though he had already experienced something, he still had to go on for eight months—loosening the kernels. Similarly, even though everything is already complete, or as we say, everyone already has Buddha nature, we still, while maintaining this view, have to pound the rice to loosen the kernels. Even though the grain has been ripe a long time, you must pound the rice, loosen the kernels, and polish the rice with that fundamental clarity. This is sometimes referred to in the Korean Zen tradition as sudden enlightenment followed by cultivation of the path. It is said that when the Fifth Patriarch was getting old, he made an announcement to the assembly: "It is not good for all of you to rely on my teaching alone, and soon I will be passing on. So each of you should write a poem that demonstrates your understanding and attainment. Whoever's poem is clearest, embracing the heart of the Dharma, will become my successor and get transmission."

Everyone in the monastery thought the head monk would be the successor. This monk was respected and learned, and he practiced hard. Yet he, himself, did not feel confident enough to present a poem directly to the Fifth Patriarch, although he knew he should compose one. So he did, and wrote it on the wall where it could be seen. The poem, which we discussed in the first chapter, said:

> The body [*this body, itself*] is the Bodhi tree [*the tree of wisdom; the Bodhi tree is the tree under which Buddha practiced*],
> The mind is the clear mirror's stand.
> Constantly we should clean them, so that no dust collects.

The Fifth Patriarch saw it and said, "This is a wonderful poem. If everyone practices according to this poem, his practice will go a long way." But he never added, "Therefore, you will be my successor." He left that ambiguous, just saying, "This is a wonderful poem." Everybody memorized the poem and talked about it.

One day Hui-neng came in from the rice-pounding shed and asked about this poem. Because he had been poor and needed to support his mother, he had had no time to go to school, so he could neither read nor write. Someone recited the poem for him, and as he heard the words he realized it was a good poem, but that it did not go to the heart of Zen Dharma. According to the story, he then composed his own poem, asking some other young novice to write it on the wall, next to the other one. His poem said:

> Bodhi has no tree.
> The clear mirror has no stand.
> Originally nothing.
> Where is dust?

There is a very different spirit to this poem. The other one is about gradual cultivation, developing something, polishing, polishing. This one says all of that is only your idea, your conceptualization, and your imagining something. Before all that,

Bodhi has no tree, clear mirror has no stand, originally nothing. Don't dwell anywhere, let the mind come forth. Where can you find dust? If you see things from this point of view, there is no defilement anywhere. Everything is bright and shining, expressing itself as the truth. From this perspective live your life.

When the Fifth Patriarch read this poem, he understood the heart of it, but did not openly acknowledge it. Because he understood the politics of the monastery, he had it erased. In the middle of the night he called the rice pounder to his room, where he transmitted the teachings of the *Diamond Sutra* and gave him the formal dharma robe and bowl, the signs of Zen transmission. He also warned him, "The monks here will never tolerate your being given transmission." The rice pounder, after all, was not even a monk. Moreover, he was illiterate and from the south of China, where the northerners considered everyone to be a barbarian. The Fifth Patriarch continued, "You should take the robe and bowl, and flee." Some versions of the story say the Fifth Patriarch even rowed him across the river and sent him on his way, telling him to stay in hiding for some years while cultivating his realization more fully.

The last lines of the poem tell that story:

> In the middle of the night, he entered the fifth patriarch's
>   room
> The fifth patriarch personally passed on to him the
>   Dharma robe
> [*Due to the jealousy of other followers of the Fifth Patriarch*]
> His life was hanging by a thread
> So he secretly crossed the West River by moonlight

Then the final line, an interesting line, reads:

> Who knew at that time?—he was glad to leave

Sometimes we finish some segment of our own journey; something is transmitted to us. Dharma transmission is not just the passing of this robe back and forth; it is ongoing, moment by moment by moment. There is always something transmitting its teaching to us. Some circumstances of our lives are greater teachers than others. Some are momentary. Others have deep impact and unfold over time. But sometimes, even after we have had some experience and the meaning has been transmitted to us, we fail to let go; we do not allow completion of that facet of our life's journey.

T'aego says, "Who knew at that time?—he was glad to leave." That means he completely let go at that time. We must also be able to see that when it happens to us and be glad to leave.

The next day the Fifth Patriarch did not give his dharma speech. The day after that, he again failed to give one. The monks asked, "Why are you not giving your dharma speech any longer?"

He said, "The Dharma has left here." Then he told them, "The lay brother in the rice shed has been given the robe and bowl, and has gone. He is now my successor."

They could not believe it! A group of them went after him to bring back the robe and bowl, both sacred relics. One monk—who had been an army general before retiring and becoming a monk—was really fired up about this. Some versions of the story characterize him as arrogant and aggressive; others, as simple and almost naïve and guileless. But his intensity here was one-pointed, and he finally caught up to the Sixth Patriarch. When he saw this monk coming, the Sixth Patriarch put the robe and the bowl on the ground, and said, "This robe and this bowl are the symbols of dharma transmission. They are the point of our faith, so they should not be fought over. Take them if you want." But when the monk went to pick them up, he could not budge them. Perhaps he recognized that they did not belong to him and froze in a conflict of some kind.

At that point, the monk had a sudden change himself. His eyes, too, switched around. He said, "I have not come for the robe and the bowl, I have come for the dharma teaching. Please teach me, lay brother."

The Sixth Patriarch replied, "Don't make good and bad. At that moment, what is your original face before your parents were born?" When the monk heard that, he had an awakening.

This monk shows us an interesting kind of strong energy practice mind. Sometimes we, too, can be going 180 degrees in the wrong direction, but if our dedication is strong something can suddenly wake us up, even if we are completely ass-backwards. When you have a strong intensity of energy directed toward something, you can experience a sudden shift and perceive something. This monk had an awakening at that moment. Then he asked, "Besides these secret teachings that you've just revealed to me, are there any higher secret teachings?"

In his commentary on this case, Robert Aitken Roshi, an American Zen master who teaches in Hawaii, once described this monk as something like a chick: When chicks come out of an egg, sometimes—even though they are out—you still see a few pieces of eggshell sticking to them. So, even though the monk came out at that moment, still there was a little something sticking to him. Then he asked, "Is there something more than this? Something more secret?"

I looked up the word *secret* in the dictionary. In my house, two people use the dictionary: I look up words used in Zen teaching; my son looks up words for his rap lyrics. I am not sure which of us is more to the point! One of the meanings of secrecy, after the fourth definition, is closeness, which implies intimacy. So in this story we might say that the monk is asking, "After this that you have revealed to me, is there anything even more intimate than this?"

The Sixth Patriarch replied, "What I have just revealed to you is not secret at all. If you turn around and perceive the face of your true self, then everything is already there. Take good care of the Dharma and only go straight." That means, even after you have some perception like that, take good care of it, cultivate it, and only go straight moment by moment by moment.

That story appears in the *Mu Mun Kwan* [Chin., *Wu-men-kuan*; Jap., *Mumonkan*], one of the most important collections of kong-ans in Zen literature. At the end of the case, Mu Mun [Chin., Wu-men; Jap., Mumon] has a little poem:

> Cannot envision, cannot paint.
> Cannot praise. Put it all down!
> Nowhere to hide the original face.
> When the universe collapses, it does not decay![2]

"Nowhere to hide the original face" means it is there when you stand up, there when you sit down, there in the midst of your crying, there as you laugh, there in deep sadness, there in great joy. Even in the hiding of it, it is there in the hiding. There is nowhere that it cannot be seen.

I hope we all look into the journey of the Sixth Patriarch and realize that we, too, are on the rice-pounding treadmill. And that the rice has been ripe for a long time.

THE
MODERN
PERIOD

Zen Master

Kyong Ho and

His Successors

THE TEACHINGS OF KYONG HO

Perceive the way and you attain a point of safety and
*   anchorage.*
Enter the way and you attain the realm of danger and
*   lose your life.*
Safety and danger, life and death; all come from where?
. . . .
The activity of the great ones is, when hanging over a
*   cliff one thousand feet high, to be able to let go.*
Yaahh!

The history of Korean Zen can be viewed as a series of renewals and declines. Periodically, some great master would appear and infuse the teaching and tradition with energy, but gradually this energy would dissipate. This was the situation until Zen Master T'aego unified the Nine Mountains Schools into the Chogye Order, which resulted in a period of lasting vitality. His transmission line has remained unbroken. The next great master on the scene was Sosan Taesa (1520–1604), whose *Handbook for Zen Students* has exerted a strong influence on practitioners down to the present day. After Sosan and his immediate successors died, Buddhism in Korea was actively opposed by the government, and for the next three hundred years Zen practice was no longer widespread except in the mountains, where Zen monks continued to keep their tradition alive. Then Zen Master Kyong Ho appeared.

Kyong Ho, who was born in 1849 and died in 1912, played a major role in reviving the Zen tradition in Korean Buddhism. Born into a poor family, he was about nine when his father died. Mother and child then went to live in a temple. That was a custom at that time: Those who could not support themselves could live in a temple. It is likely that Kyong Ho's mother served as a helper in the temple, while Kyong Ho became a novice monk there.

Kyong Ho proved to be extremely bright, a child prodigy. Over the next several years he was exposed to all the traditional Buddhist teachings, as well as to the Confucianist and Taoist teachings, and he learned to read classical Chinese. By the time he was twenty-one he was already quite famous throughout Korea for the extent of his learning.

At age twenty-three, Kyong Ho was appointed to the post of scriptural teacher of Buddhism, perhaps the equivalent of a lecturer or professor in our university system, and kept that position until he was about thirty. At that point, something radical happened in his life, changing the whole course of events. It is a famous story in the Korean Zen tradition.

Kyong Ho had decided to take a short vacation trip to Seoul, where he planned to visit a former teacher. As he passed through a village on the way, he was caught in a severe storm and sought refuge in a small house. As he entered the house, he found it filled with dead bodies and soon realized that everybody in the village had died of cholera. Suddenly Kyong Ho had an insight into the impermanence of life and recognized that while he understood the teachings about impermanence, he had not attained Buddha's mind because he was quite fearful.

Kyong Ho aborted his trip and returned to the temple, where he resigned his position as lecturer. He moved to a small hermitage on the temple grounds and began practicing intensive meditation. The story goes that Kyong Ho was practicing so rigorously that his fellow monks would bring him food every day so he could sit all day long. When Kyong Ho got sleepy he would stick himself in the leg with a sharp object to wake himself up.

One day, about three months after Kyong Ho had begun his retreat, the novice monk who would bring his food went into town, where he ran into a layman who knew Kyong Ho. The layman asked, "What is the great teacher Kyong Ho doing these days? I heard that he resigned his teaching post."

The novice monk replied, "Yes, Kyong Ho is practicing very, very hard. He only sits, eats, and lies down."

At that, the layman said, "If he only sits, eats, and lies down, Kyong Ho will be reborn as a cow."

Now, to follow this story, you have to know about a traditional Buddhist teaching that says, "When a monk dies he is reborn as a cow with no nostrils." But the novice did not relate to this and got upset at the layman's remark. "Kyong Ho is one of the greatest Buddhist teachers in all Korea," he declared. "How can you say he will be born again as a cow?"

The layman replied, "No, that's not the way to respond to my question. What you should have said is, 'If Kyong Ho is reborn as a cow, will he be born as a cow with no nostrils?'" Still not comprehending, the monk went back to Kyong Ho, knocked on the door and told the story. When Kyong Ho heard the line "born as a cow with no nostrils," his mind suddenly opened and he ended his retreat.

Another translation of that line reads, "though I be reborn as a cow there is no place for the reins." In Asia cows or oxen are tethered through the nose, so having "no place for the reins" is an image of freedom: If you have no reins you cannot be pulled this way and that. If the ox represents mind, that means your mind is completely free.

Although Kyong Ho's awakening experience was confirmed by his teacher, Master Manhwa, Kyong Ho was not satisfied. He felt his enlightenment was not yet steady enough. He moved to another temple—actually, the one where his mother was staying—and practiced even more rigorously for the next two years. By then he was thirty-three and finally felt satisfied with the steadiness of his attainment. His attainment was certified by the temple's Zen master, Vongam, and Kyong Ho was given the title of Zen master. Shortly after that he assumed the post as head priest of the temple, where he stayed until he was about forty.

Then Kyong Ho was suddenly lit with the fire of missionary spirit. He began traveling all over Korea, staying in all the main temples, and encouraging and inspiring monks and nuns to practice Zen meditation. He also started a community movement to bring together monks, nuns, and laypeople. At the time he was considered the premier monk in all Korea. But one day, at the age of fifty-six, he just disappeared, right at the height of his career. He went to live in a remote fishing village somewhere in the northern part of Korea. He stopped wearing monk's clothes, stopped shaving his head, and began teaching illiterate children in the village to read. From time to time he would hire himself out as a farm hand, or mingle with villagers, discussing politics and situations in the world. In his sixty-fourth year, he called two of his main disciples to the village and recited a poem he had composed:

Light from the moon of clear mind
drinks up everything in the world.
When mind and light disappear,
What . . . is . . . this . . . ?[1]

Shortly after that, he died.

One commentator on Kyong Ho's life says his teaching can
be viewed from three perspectives: his teaching about Zen, his
teaching about the sense of community, and his own demonstration of the Zen ox-herding pictures (a traditional set of ten
calligraphic illustrations that portray the different stages in the
journey to complete realization). You can see different aspects
of these three strands in a poem he composed in his early thir-
ties. Presented below are some sections of this poem. In it, you
can hear a tone of lament and perceive that something is stirring
in him—something that later becomes the urge to act and teach
more widely. The poem is called "The Song of Enlightenment"[2]:

I look around in all directions,
   but cannot find anyone to whom I may transmit my *kasa*
      and bowl.
Oh, I can find no one!

In the Buddhist tradition the *kasa* (a biblike garment one
wears after taking precepts) and the bowl are formally passed
on from Zen master to successor. So on one level Kyong Ho is
saying, "When I look around, I can't find anyone who seems to
be interested in my teaching," reflecting the dilapidated state of
Buddhism, especially of Zen, in Korea at that time. But on another level, I think on a more profound level, he is saying,
"When I look around in any direction, I can't find any other, so
there is no one to transmit anything to and there is nothing to
be transmitted." Then he goes on:

Oh, I can find no one!

In spring, flowers are in full bloom in the mountain.

In autumn the moon is bright and the wind is cool.

I sing a song of no birth,

but who will ever listen to my song?

My life and fate, what shall I do?

There is a story that when Shakyamuni Buddha attained enlightenment under the Bodhi tree, he debated for seven days what he was going to do, because he felt he would not be able to communicate his realization to anyone. According to the legend, all the gods and bodhisattvas came and implored him to teach in the world. Then he devised strategies through which to teach. This poem by Kyong Ho has a similar flavor. He says that the spring flowers and the autumn moon—everything—reveal the song of no birth. But, "Who will ever listen to my song? . . . What shall I do?" Then he goes further:

The color of the mountain is the eye of

Avalokitesvara Bodhisattva [*the bodhisattva of great*
compassion]

The sound of the river is the ear of the Manjushri

Bodhisattva [*the bodhisattva of great wisdom*].

Mr. Chang and Mrs. Lee are Vairochana Buddha.

Mr. Chang and Mrs. Lee is like saying "Mr. Smith and Mrs. Jones," and *Vairochana Buddha* means the "great universal Buddha of light." This "light" has two aspects: the universal light, the one light that covers everything, and the light that is shining in every particular form and existence in the world. So Kyong Ho is saying that Mr. Smith and Mrs. Jones are the Buddha of Great Light. He continues:

Sentient beings call on Buddha or patriarch, Zen or Kyo
    [*sutras*],
But in origin, all of them are one.
The stone man blows the flute and the wooden man
    sleeps,
But the common man does not realize his own mind.
And they like to call it a holy land!
What nonsense!
What a pity!

Further on, he says:

Hearing someone say "A cow without nostrils,"
I realized the true mind,
Where there is no name nor form.
I radiate great light in all directions.
The single bright light on the forehead is the Pure Land.
The divine form around the head is God's world.
Four *skandhas* [*the aggregates of attachment*] are pure body.
Paradise is the hell of boiling cauldron and the hell of cold
    water;
Heavenly world is the hell of sword-trees and sword-
    mountains;
Buddha Land is a heap of dry dung;
The triple world is an anthill;
Trikaya [*the three bodies*] is emptiness.
Wherever you touch, there is the heavenly truth.
Oh, how wonderful! How miraculous!

There is a story about the Japanese Zen Master Ikkyu taking
a boat somewhere. On the boat with him was a monk who
practiced one of the esoteric forms of meditation found in Japan

at that time, maybe Taoist or Tantric meditation, something connected with trying to get extraordinary powers and supernatural experiences. This monk chided Ikkyu, "Oh, you Zen monks don't attain anything special."

When the boat got to the dock and a gangway was put in place, a dog stood near it, barking fiercely. The monk immediately took out his prayer beads and started rolling them and chanting a mantra, trying to calm the dog. But Ikkyu simply walked down the ramp, took out a rice cake, handed it to the dog, patted him on the head, and walked on. "Wherever you touch, there is the heavenly truth. Oh, how wonderful, how miraculous!"

> The wind is cool through the pine trees, everywhere is
>   blue mountain.
> The moon is bright in autumn, the sky is like water.
> Yellow flower and green bamboo, canary-song and
>   swallow-sound.
> In all these, there is Great Function.
> The golden crown of a worldly king is but the thorny
>   crown of the prisoner;
> The Diamond Seal of a heavenly king is but an eyeball of
>   a skull.
> Countless Buddhas are always manifest in grass, trees,
>   stones;
> The Avatamsaka and Lotus Sutras are but my walking,
>   staying, sitting and lying.
> To say there is no Buddha and no Bodhisattva is no
>   nonsense;
> To change hell into heaven,
> That is in my power.
> Thousands of sermons and thousands of secret meanings

Are realized on waking up from sleep and they are in full
    bloom before my eyes.
Where can I find time and space?

He continues:

There is nothing right, wrong, good or bad;
The ignorant, hearing this, call me a liar and do not believe
    me;
But the enlightened believe me and do not doubt,
And they will attain Nirvana.

Then he ends the poem:

To whom shall I transmit my *kasa* and bowl?
I can't find anyone in any direction.

Kyong Ho's specific teachings on Zen are connected with
two things. First, he revitalized the method of focusing with
one big question, called *hwadu* in Korean, which literally means
"wordhead." If you pick one big question—such as "What am
I?" or "What is mind?"—the spirit of that question points you
toward the place from which all words and speech appear and
disappear. Kyong Ho revitalized the tradition of holding one big
question and practicing with it, no matter what you were doing,
whether it was sitting or walking or eating or working or resting
at leisure—just keeping that question, always. This tradition had
existed in Korea for many centuries, but at that time in the late
1800s, even though people knew about it, the actual practice
and effort had pretty much died out. Kyong Ho encouraged
people to practice it again.

The second aspect of his teaching was his view of what he
called "practice/enlightenment." He used a simile, saying that
practice and enlightenment are like the front and the back of

your hand. That is an interesting image, because the front of your hand is not the back of your hand, and the back of your hand is different from the front of your hand. But wherever the front of your hand goes, it does not go without the back of your hand. And wherever the back of your hand goes, it does not go there without the front. So wherever there is practice, there is also enlightenment. And wherever there is enlightenment, there is practice. Sometimes you see the front of the hand. It can do many things: pick up objects, manipulate things, and be active. But sometimes suddenly you get hit with the back of the hand. Then you get quite an awakening. Kyong Ho's view of practice/enlightenment means, essentially, that when you practice something sincerely, with one hundred percent effort and without making any distinctions, at that time enlightenment is already there.

Recently the Providence Zen Center newsletter featured an article, "The Great Matter of Life and Death, Zen Master Kyong Ho,"[3] that included his teachings on meditation. The article has two sections: the first presents a series of Kyong Ho's admonitions, designed to chide people into practicing sincerely; the second focuses on his teachings about keeping a questioning attitude.

I am going to paraphrase some of this article. Kyong Ho is addressing monks and nuns, but his points could apply equally to anyone who is trying to practice a life of nonclinging and nonattachment. His admonitions begin in a classical way:

> It is no small thing for a person to become a monk or a nun. The person does not become a monk to eat and dress well.

Sometimes in Asian countries, people who had no access to the main rungs of society would enter a monastery as a way of taking an alternate route. There you were fed, clothed, and treated fairly decently. But Kyong Ho says a person does not become a monk to eat and dress well. Instead, a person does so because he or she wants to be free from life and death by accomplishing Buddhahood.

Then Kyong Ho exorts his students to be serious and to cultivate a one-pointed questioning:

> To accomplish Buddhahood, one has to discover one's own mind, which is already within one's own body. To discover mind, one should understand that one's body is no more than a dead corpse, and that this world is, for good or bad, nothing more than a dream. One's death is like popping out in the evening of the same day that you were popped in during the same morning. After death, sometimes you may be born into one of the hells; sometimes in the realm of animals, and sometimes in the realm of ghosts. [*Not just after death; maybe five times a day you will find yourself in one of the hells. If you are running after something without having your mind intact, you are in the realm of ghosts.*]
>
> Then one must endure incalculable pains and sufferings. Since this is true, do not concern yourself with the worldly life. Just examine and carefully observe your mind at all times. What does this which is now seeing, hearing and thinking look like? [*So that is the big question: What does this which is just now seeing and hearing and thinking look like? What is it? Does it have any form or not? Is it big or small, is it yellow or green, is it bright or dark?*]
>
> Examine and observe this matter carefully. Let your examination and observation become like a mouse-catching cat, like an egg-laying hen, like a desperately hungry, old,

crafty mouse gnawing a hole in a rice bag. Let your exami-
nation and observation be focused at one point and do not
forget it. Keep it before you by raising doubt and by questioning yourself.

Doubt is not used here in the way we usually use it. The
words of the question are one thing, but the *feeling* of the question—which is, in essence, wordless—is what is meant by *doubt*.
Perplexity might be an alternate rendering. What is this that sees
and hears and thinks? *That* feeling is doubt, that attitude. We
also call it *don't-know*. Kyong Ho says:

> Do not let this doubt go while you are doing chores or the
> like. Do not let your question and doubt escape from you
> even while you are not doing anything special. By eagerly
> and sincerely practicing in this manner, finally there will
> be a moment of awakening in your own mind. Study hard
> by raising your faith. Raising your faith is sincerely re-ex-
> amining the matter just mentioned. To be born as a
> human is most difficult. It is even more difficult to be born
> into favorable circumstances; harder still to become a
> monk or nun. It is the most difficult thing of all to find
> correct and righteous dharma teaching. We should reflect
> on this matter deeply.

That is his instruction on Zen practice.

I mentioned earlier that when Kyong Ho was in his early
forties he started a community movement in Korea, modeled
somewhat on earlier movements that had existed in China during the early days of Zen and in Korea during the twelfth century. He saw coming together as a community and practicing
together as a means of "attaining the enlightenment of all bodhisattvas." He had two emphases in this community practice.

One was that meditation and wisdom should be practiced simultaneously. That is the Zen credo here: We do not practice meditation now and get wisdom later. The actual practice of Zen is meditation and wisdom together, something like his image of the front and back of the hands. Meditation means stabilizing attention and mind, becoming steady; wisdom means the expression of that through clear perceiving. They are simultaneous.

The other emphasis was stated like this: "Since we are all good dharma friends, let us practice sincerely and all attain enlightenment together."

This is an interesting statement, "Since we are all good dharma friends. . . ." When you practice in a group, the people with whom you come in contact might not be those with whom you would choose to associate on an everyday, social level, but somehow, on a dharma level, you are all close friends. On a personality level, you might not even like some of the people in the sangha. But still, on a dharma level there is something called dharma friendship. On a more profound level, it supercedes all your likes and dislikes. Kyong Ho emphasized that point in his statement.

The spirit of this community movement was inclusive in two different respects. He invited monks, nuns, laymen, laywomen, old, young, the intelligentsia, the uneducated—it did not make any difference. Anyone who sincerely wanted to practice was welcome. He only insisted that they try to cultivate a spirit of determination and involvement and a feeling of altruism. Also, his view of practice was quite broad and inclusive. Even though he, himself, was a Zen monk, he saw all different methods of practice as being equal. If someone was practicing a mantra, that was okay; if someone was practicing chanting, that was okay; if someone's practice was studying the sutras, that was okay. He only insisted that the person should practice hard and that he or she should not discriminate between different kinds of practice. No one practice was better than another.

There was one more point that Kyong Ho emphasized in this community movement: a distinction between what he considered the outer, spatial aspect and the inner attitude.

Spatial aspects of practice refer to our coming together in a particular space to practice. Because we are in a space together, we are also together at a particular time; we have a schedule. That is the outer aspect of practice.

The inner attitude, he said, is not limited by time and space. If the inner attitude of the person is sincere, according to Kyong Ho, it does not make any difference whether he or she is able to come to the place at the correct time or not. Or if a person comes there once every year, or once every five years. If we have that inner feeling that we are practicing together, then we are all dharma friends and attain enlightenment together. Then we are at one with the community.

I think that is an important point for all of us who practice in certain situations, such as practicing in a big, busy city. In some way the inner attitude of practice and of connection with community is more important than the outer spatial and time aspects.

Maybe another story will help explain this idea. Several years ago, two of my dharma brothers, Zen Master Su Bong and Zen Master Ji Bong (Bob Moore), were living on the West Coast. Su Bong was a monk and free spirit by temperament. Bob Moore is a family person; he has children and is a professor of music at the University of Southern California, with many, many responsibilities. While Su Bong used to go and do long solo retreats, Bob Moore was never able to, because of his responsibilities. Once in a talk he said, "Whenever Su Bong would go to do a long solo retreat, I would say to myself, 'I'm going to do the retreat with Su Bong.'" For however long Su Bong was in retreat—ninety days or forty-nine, whatever—Bob Moore would feel, "I'm practicing along with Su Bong in retreat." This is called the inner aspect of community, which is not hindered by time or space.

His idea has actually become institutionalized at the Providence Zen Center, as part of the traditional ninety-day winter retreat called *Kyol Che*, which means "tight practicing period." Simultaneous with the formal retreat is a practice designated as *Heart Kyol Che*, a time when those who cannot sit the retreat are encouraged to be a part of it in their hearts by pledging to do a little more intense practice on their own. Those who do that extra practice are even encouraged to come to the retreat's opening and closing ceremonies as if they were retreat members. This is an inner aspect of practice in terms of community.

The third aspect of Kyong Ho's teaching was connected with the tradition of the ox-herding pictures. In China, toward the end of the Sung dynasty (960–1279), somebody made a series of ten pictures using the ox as a representation of the mind and the ox herder as the person who is doing Buddhist practicing. The first picture is called "Searching for the Ox." Then there are titles such as "Seeing the Footprints of the Ox," "Grabbing the Reins of the Ox," "Taming the Ox," "Riding the Ox," "Ox Forgotten, Man Stands Alone." The final title is "Appearing in the Market Place with Helping Hands." For Kyong Ho, the practice of Zen was ultimately oriented toward appearing in the marketplace with helping hands. For us that means the last word of Zen is: "How do I keep my mind in daily life and manifest the original freedom of the true human being?" That was Kyong Ho's emphasis in his Zen teaching and in his Zen practice.

Kyong Ho was a colorful and unpredictable character. A couple of anecdotes will give the flavor of how he taught. One day he and his disciple Man Gong were on a begging expedition among the laypeople. At that time they were probably living in a small hermitage, maybe just the two of them, so they had to gather rice, which they would take back to the temple. The day had been good for them and the rice bag was quite full. They alternated carrying it, but because Man Gong was the student and Kyong Ho was the teacher, it was only right that Man Gong should carry the rice bag on his back more than Kyong Ho. When it was getting late in the afternoon, they were still quite a distance from their temple. Kyong Ho walked faster and faster, and Man Gong, with the rice bag on his back, complained about how heavy it was, how fast Kyong Ho was walking, and how he could not keep up. As they passed through a tiny village, a young woman came out of a building carrying a water jug on her head. She was walking toward Kyong Ho and their paths were about to meet. Just as they did, Kyong Ho grabbed her and kissed her passionately on the lips. The woman was startled. The water jug fell to the ground and smashed, and the woman ran back into the house. Within a few seconds, aunts, uncles, brothers, sisters, father, mother—everyone—charged out of the house with clubs and sticks. Kyong Ho and Man Gong ran as fast as they could; it was each for his own life. They got past the edge of town—*barely*—and the villagers finally gave up the chase. Then Kyong Ho and Man Gong stood there—huffing and puffing. Kyong Ho looked at Man Gong, and with a slight smile on his lips he said, "Sunim (an honorific used in addressing a monk or nun), is that rice bag heavy?"

Man Gong replied, "What's heavy? I didn't even know I had it on my back. And we ran so far."

Kyong Ho then said, "Aren't you lucky to have me as your

teacher? Before, you had heavy in your mind, but now you've attained no-heavy."

Another time, Kyong Ho and Man Gong were out somewhere together and got caught in a downpour. They took shelter in some kind of man-made, cavelike structure, probably made out of big boulders cemented together. As they sat there, Kyong Ho kept looking up at the ceiling every couple of seconds. This began to make Man Gong feel uneasy. Finally he said to his teacher, "Master, how come you keep looking up at that big rock up there?"

Kyong Ho replied, "I'm afraid it might fall."

Man Gong looked puzzled, then asked, "How is that big rock going to fall?"

Kyong Ho said, "The safest place is the most dangerous."

That is Kyong Ho's teaching: The safest place is the most dangerous.

Not surprisingly, Kyong Ho is known in the Korean Zen tradition for his pithiness: "Don't wish for perfect health; in perfect health there is greed and wanting. An ancient once said, 'Make good medicine from the suffering of sickness.'" That second sentence is worth looking at. When I first met Zen Master Seung Sahn he was in his early- to mid-40s and already had severe diabetes. People occasionally would say to him, "Diabetes, that's a terrible disease," expressing their concern and sympathy. He always replied, "No, no, diabetes is very good"—as if to say, make good medicine out of your sickness; find teaching in everything. Kyong Ho says, "Don't hope for a life without problems. An easy life results in a judgmental and lazy mind. An ancient once said, 'Accept the anxieties and difficulties of this life.'"

Kyong Ho made another statement, one that is important to us: "Don't expect your practice to be always clear of obstacles.

Without hindrances, the mind that seeks enlightenment may be burnt out. An ancient once said, 'Attain deliverance in disturbance.'" That means, if you do not have something to push against, you have no resistance, so you lose strength. If you have something to push against, then you gain power.

Kyong Ho also said, "Don't expect to practice hard and not experience the weird. Hard practice that evades the unknown makes for a weak commitment. An ancient once said, 'Help hard practice by befriending every demon.'"

So do not think that your practice should always be clear of obstacles, because, in fact, obstacles help you gain power.

ZEN MASTER MAN GONG'S
"OUT OF THE NET"

If you attain zero point, you have already passed through
and are free.
If you attach to zero point, you are like a monkey who
sticks its hand in a jar to pull out a piece of fruit, but
finds that its hand, when holding the fruit, is too big
to get out of the jar; so you become stuck.
If you pass beyond "free" and "stuck" then what
becomes clear?

. . . .

Birds fly, feathers fall;
Fish swim, the water gets muddy.

Zen Master Man Gong was perhaps the greatest and most well known successor to Kyong Ho. Man Gong was born in 1872 and passed away in 1946 just after the end of the Second World War. He furthered Kyong Ho's intention of encouraging a wide practice community by teaching Zen to laypeople and to nuns as well as to monks. At the time this was considered radical. In fact, four of Man Gong's dharma successors were nuns.

Man Gong became a monk when he was a boy. At first he studied the sutras at Dong Hak Sa, the temple where Kyong Ho had been a sutra master before his conversion to Zen. At the age of thirteen Man Gong met Kyong Ho; the occasion was a ceremony at the temple to mark the end of the year's sutra study and the beginning of vacation. At the ceremony the current sutra master gave a speech in which he encouraged the students to become like great trees from which temples are built, and like great bowls of dharma; he also instructed them to avoid bad company and to always keep the Buddha in mind.

Then Kyong Ho, who was visiting the temple, spoke. He said:

> All of you are monks. Monks are free of petty personal attachments, and live only to serve all people. Wanting to become a great tree or container of the Dharma will prevent you from becoming a true teacher. Great trees have great uses; small trees have small uses. Good and bad bowls can all be used in their own ways. None is to be discarded. Keep both good and bad friends. You mustn't reject anything. This is true Buddhism. My only wish is that you free yourselves from all conceptual thinking.

Man Gong was so impressed that he asked Kyong Ho to take him with him and accept him as a student. Kyong Ho at first refused, but then, glimpsing Man Gong's potential and sincerity, agreed.

Man Gong studied hard for the next five years. At the age of eighteen he heard the kong-an: "The ten thousand dharmas return to the one: Where does the one return to?" He was immediately seized by a feeling of great doubt and could not think of anything else. He worked with the question for several years until he had an initial enlightenment while chanting the words of the morning bell chant, "If you wish to understand all Buddhas of the past, present, and future, you must perceive that the whole universe is created by mind alone." As he hit the bell, his mind opened and he understood that all Buddhas dwell in a single sound.

Man Gong was elated, but he began to lose his balanced and clear perception. He became attached to "The whole universe is one. I am Buddha!" and began erroneously to see himself as a free man without any hindrances. Kyong Ho had to work patiently with him, using both grandmotherly compassion and sternness, to dislodge Man Gong's attachment to emptiness and freedom so as to bring him to perceive Zen as everyday mind and ordinariness. Kyong Ho further emphasized that Man Gong's practice should be rooted in altruism and compassion— what we might refer to as practice for the sake of all beings.

There are a few anecdotes that refer to this phase of Man Gong's training and refinement of his bodhisattva vow. Once, when Man Gong visited his teacher on his birthday, he said to him, "You already have everything, but I have brought you a gift of some food." Then Man Gong took out some meat, wine, and rice cakes. Now, according to strict observance of the Buddhist precepts, monks should not eat meat or drink wine.

Kyong Ho just said, "Oh wonderful! Where did you get all this?"

To which Man Gong replied, "Nowadays I have no hindrance. If someone gives me wine, I drink. If they don't, I don't drink. If someone gives me meat, I eat. Meat and rice are the same. If rice cakes come, I eat rice cakes."

Then Kyong Ho said, "Oh, Man Gong Sunim, you are wonderful. But my mind is not this style."

"Then Master, what is your style?" asked Man Gong.

"I cannot get freedom. I want something." This is an interesting remark. It means that if your practice is rooted in the great vow for all beings, then you still have a want—for others.

Then one can use "good and bad"; it becomes a desire for universal good.

Kyong Ho continued, "For example, perhaps I want some garlic. In the temple there is no garlic, so I go to the city and buy some. Instead of eating it immediately, I put it into the ground on my return to the temple. Soon it grows and a lot of garlic appears. Then I eat some."

On hearing this, Man Gong's mind opened. He said, "Zen Master, I am sorry. Before I didn't understand, but now I see that my practice has been only about me, and an attachment to freedom."

On another occasion, when Man Gong was serving as his teacher's attendant, a woman in an advanced state of leprosy knocked on the door begging alms. Kyong Ho reached out and took the woman's hand, and led her into his room. And there she stayed for three days. Kyong Ho gave instructions to Man Gong to leave food for two outside his door, and not to disturb him. When the woman left, Man Gong said to Kyong Ho, "You are my teacher, and I don't question your actions . . ." but he gave an inquisitive look to his teacher, who as a monk had taken a vow of celibacy.

Kyong Ho responded, "When I first saw this woman with her outstretched arms begging for alms, I perceived that she had almost lost touch with any human feeling or warmth. So I took her by the hand and stayed with her in my room for three days." A Catholic priest on hearing this story observed, "Ah, Kyong Ho even renounced his holiness!"

Now let us move on to Man Gong as a teacher. In the Zen tradition, images are sometimes used as teaching devices. Sometimes the meanings of those images are fairly evident; at other times they may need some explanation. For example, the ox often represents mind—not something you would know automatically. Probably old Chinese masters chose the ox because you have to tend an ox, you have to train it; likewise, you have to train your mind and discipline it in the practice of Zen. The full moon also may represent mind. When Zen poets write poems about looking at the full moon and appreciating it, they often are simultaneously talking about the moon and about the mind, with its luminous, shining quality.

Man Gong is associated with a kong-an that uses another image: a net. This is a far more obvious image. The following presentation of this traditional kong-an comes from Zen Master Seung Sahn's collection, *The Whole World Is a Single Flower*, which contains 365 kong-ans. This is Case 12, "How Do You Get Out of the Net?"[1]:

> One day, Zen Master Man Gong sat on the high seat rostrum and gave the Hae Jae Dharma speech to mark the end of the three-month winter Kyol Che. "All of you sat in the Dharma Room for three months. That is very, very wonderful. As for me, I only stayed in my room making a net. This net is made from a special string. It is very strong and can catch Buddha, Dharma, Bodhisattvas, human beings—everything. How do you get out of this net?"

As I mentioned in the last chapter, in the Korean Zen tradition monks and nuns sit a three-month winter retreat called *Kyol Che*. At the conclusion of the retreat, the Zen master who has been presiding gives a formal dharma speech from the high seat. Then they have a relaxed period called *Hae Jae*.

In this case, Man Gong mounts the rostrum and says, "All of you sat in the dharma room for three months. That is very, very wonderful." That means, "You did hard training, were sincere, and exerted yourselves." That is not a commonplace thing, it is wonderful. "As for me," he continued, "I only stayed in my room making a net." In other words, "During the whole three months, while you all stayed in the dharma room practicing sitting meditation for many hours a day, I only stayed in my room making a net." He concludes by asking, "How will all of you get out of this net?"

The case continues:

> Some students shouted, "KATZ!" Others hit the floor, or raised a fist, or said, "The sky is blue, the tree is green." One said, "Already got out. How are you, great Zen Master?" while another shouted from the back of the room, "Don't make net!"
>
> Many answers were given, but to each Man Gong only responded, "Aha! I've caught a big fish!"

This gives you a flavor of traditional Zen—sometimes the Zen master and the assembly would have these lively interactions. Most people picture a Zen interview as something private: You go to the Zen master's room, have a short interchange, then go out. But in the old traditions of China and Korea, they would often have lively public interchanges, with different people responding in the moment.

At the end of the case, Zen Master Seung Sahn writes a commentary:

> Don't make anything. If you make something, then something is a hindrance. The sky is always bright. Clouds appear and the sky is dark. The wind blows and the clouds disappear. When you put down your opinions and conditions, the correct situation, correct relationship and correct function will appear. If you are attached to speech and words then you are already dead. Be careful.
>
> Understand that to return to primary point, you must begin at 0°, go around the circle, and return to 360°.

He doesn't say, "Don't use words and speech"—that words and speech are no good, or irrelevant, or anything like that. He only says, if you get attached to words and speech, then you deaden your original vitality and aliveness and brightness. So you are already dead. Be careful.

Man Gong has set this up as a device to test his students at the end of the three-month retreat. He says, "I just sat making a net, and it's made of very, very special string," because it is possible—just as you can get attached to words and speech—to get attached to hard training and difficult practice. If you become attached to the formalities of Zen, they have the potential of becoming a hindrance and a block. Essentially, Man Gong is saying to his students, "You did hard training, but are you clear about the matter? Or have you become attached to what you just did? Have you developed some kind of subtle egotism, even, around the fact that you just sat in meditation for three months, and how special it was?"

Man Gong was very skillful at challenging and taking away his students' mental constructions and attachments. For instance, once a monk approached him and asked, "Where is the Buddha's teaching?"

Man Gong replied, "Right in front of you."

The monk then said, "You say, 'Right in front of you,' but I don't see it."

"You make *I*," answered Man Gong, "so you don't see it."

The monk asked him, "Do you see it, Master?"

Man Gong responded, "If you make *I*, it's difficult to see it. But if you make *you*, it's even more difficult to see it."

This is an interesting point: All the time we are making some constructed sense of *I* and some constructed sense of *you*. What kind of *I* do I make just now, and what kind of *you*? Practice is about perceiving that process over and over again. First we make *I* and *you*, then we begin to adorn them. That is when interesting things begin to emerge: "I am a failure, you're a success." Or, "I'm a success, you're a failure." "I'm beautiful/handsome, you're not so beautiful/handsome." And the reverse. This is putting clothes on *I* and *you*, then taking the labeling very seriously. Man Gong wrote a poem about *I* and *you*:

> Holding a bamboo stick, never stop.
> Already arrive in front of Bo Duk cave.
> Who is host, who is the guest? They cannot see each
>   other.
> Only very close by, the gurgle of the stream.[2]

The commentary states: The sound of the stream takes away both host and guest.

Now to return to Man Gong's net and the issue of hard training. More important than to do hard training is—over and over again—to perceive and let go, perceive and put it down, perceive and don't *make*, perceive and don't hold anything tightly with attachment.

Still, for those of us who are trying to practice while living in the world—not as monastics of some kind—there are three kinds of hard training that we have to engage in.

First, we should practice consistently and regularly on a daily basis. Everyone should form—and try to live by—an intention to do some formal practice every day, even if it is only ten or fifteen minutes of sitting. Regularity is very important; that is hard, hard training.

Second, we must learn to use our everyday circumstances as the field of our practice. This is difficult. The streets of New York facing us every day do not offer a rarified atmosphere like that of a mountain temple, where everything is simple, clear, and pure. You could say that, for us, the garbage in our streets is the field of *bodhi*, the field of wisdom.

Third, we all should occasionally do some hard training that tests us. Come to a retreat periodically—one day, three days, a week, forty-nine days, or a hundred days—some kind of retreat. One where you really push yourself beyond where you normally think you can go.

And we must realize that it is not only Man Gong Sunim who makes a net. We all make our personal nets, the kind that hinder and obstruct us, obscuring what is right in front of us. That is why the second great vow of the bodhisattva path says, "Delusions are endless; I vow to cut through them all." We all form these nets of special string, then ensnare ourselves and get all knotted up. Next, we begin carrying those knots around with us.

Sometimes we take those knots to a massage therapist and find that when the therapist touches them in a particular way, we get sad and start crying, or become angry, or feel fearful. Any number of things can emerge. We all hold so many things in our bodies that they become the congealed representation of our experiences. The Indian yoga and Chinese *qigong* (chi kung) traditions have techniques to undo this knottedness, using movement, breathing, and visualization. In Tibetan Buddhism they have a technique where you imagine taking in the negativity of others and sending out good thoughts to the world. Any of these techniques can be quite useful, and, to be honest, I practice some of them myself.

But there are limitations to these practices: You may be able to stretch your body and loosen the feeling of knottedness or contraction, but if you do not perceive how you mentally and emotionally make the contraction, and then practice letting go, your old condition will reappear.

The Zen way of looking at this is to perceive clearly what you are making, how you are holding, where you are attaching, what you are clinging to, and let go. Put all of that—*ptchh*—down.

In the *Hua-yen Sutra* (Skt., *Avatamsaka Sutra*), a major scripture in Buddhism, there is a poem that we teach people when they first come for individual training. I recently found two other translations of this poem besides the one we use in our tradition. There are small but interesting differences in the nuances of these translations. Our version says:

> If you want to understand the realm of Buddhas,
> Keep a mind that is clear like space.
> Let all thinking and external desires fall away.
> Let your mind go anyplace with no hindrance.[3]

Each of the others have slightly different wording. The last two lines of the second version read:

> Detaching from all appearances and fixations,
> Causing the mind to be unobstructed where it turns.[4]

Now that is an interesting phrase, "Detaching from all appearances and fixations," because "appearances" means being caught in the realm of appearances and not going to the essential, and "fixations" is where you get stuck. The final line, "Causing the mind to be unobstructed where it turns," is about activity. The last line of our version, "Let your mind go anyplace with no hindrance," gives the sense of freedom. The final line of the third version is, "Having the mind unobstructed amidst all objects," meaning unobstructed in the world. To be free and to actively move freely in the world is the essence of this poem—keeping a mind that is clear like space.

An old Zen master put it another way: "Don't go to the

branches, but go to the root." If you perceive that you are caught up in a personalized net of some kind, then go to the root. And the root is the way we are relating to our *I* sense.

We all form some sense of *I*. We already have an *I* that is adequate in itself, but we form another one. Then we dress it up: We put a top hat on it, a tuxedo, or an evening dress. Then to substantiate that *I,* we tell ourselves stories about the world—more construction and fabrication—to support that sense of *I*-ness.

But if you want to get to the root, you need to cultivate, ongoingly, "Don't-know *I*-ness." If you continuously and every-where keep "Don't-know *I*," then the mind is free and radiates in all directions; it does not hold anything.

From that point, if you practice perceiving the context out of which all of your reactions spring, you can clearly move through them. To perceive the context from which our reac-tions spring means to see the causes and conditions that drive us. If you see horns sticking up from behind a stone wall, you might infer that there is a bull back there. And if you see smoke coming from behind the hill, you could suspect there is a fire somewhere.

But sometimes we miss the "smoke" in our own personali-ties. I was talking recently with a friend of mine who has a bubbly, vivacious personality, with a curiosity about things and a sense of adventurousness—along with a tendency to overreact at times. I said to her, "You know, sometimes you're a little too reactive." Her response was, "I thought that was just my personality—you know I'm Irish."

It is true that we all have different kinds of temperaments, and out of these temperaments certain personality styles do arise. It is probably also true that different cultural groupings form certain ways of expressing themselves. But it is not enough to say, "Oh, I thought that was just my personality," and "I'm Irish." When looking at the moment-by-moment contexts in which we are interacting and reacting, we must return to the mind before reacting and perceive what it is that presses our buttons. We must discover, as Zen Master Seung Sahn used to say, "Where is the pain point?" If we perceive where that is, then we can perceive how we are reacting quickly from our pain point and can do something about it. But most of the time we hit a pain point and, without discernment, impulsively react in some way. That reactivity becomes compulsive and habitual, and we get all knotted up and ensnared in it.

One of my students told me, "I was driving down Second Avenue and the cab drivers were cutting in and out, in and out. I started to take it very personally and got furious." Then he added reflectively, "They were just being cab drivers; that's what cab drivers do in New York."

You have to look at what kind of expectations you carry and hold and react to. And you can only see that if you find a vantage point from which to look. That is why it is very important in practice to cultivate this "Don't-know I" and to perceive, moment by moment, how you are moving in the world.

Another story about a net involves an interchange between Zen Master Hsueh-feng (Jap., Seppo; Kor., Seol Bong) and Zen Master San-sheng (Jap., Sansho; Kor., Sam Seong), who was visiting Hsueh-feng's temple. San-sheng said to Hsueh-feng, "I wonder what the golden carp who has passed through the net uses for food."

Hsueh-feng said, "When you pass through the net, then I'll tell you."

That is "how two masters show their swords." After San-sheng asked his challenging question, Hsueh-feng returned with his own challenge—*ptchh*—"When *you* pass through the net, then we'll talk about it."

But San-sheng, being quite steady in himself, was not to be daunted by that and replied, "You're the teacher of 1,500 people and you don't even understand the point of my question."

So Hsueh-feng became the quintessential "old cow" of Zen at that moment and said, "This old monk is busy taking care of the temple."

It is an interesting image: San-sheng does not talk about getting *out* of the net; he says, "What is it that the golden carp who has passed *through* the net uses for food?" We are *caught* in the net when we take ourselves very seriously, when everything looks small and tight and constrained and constricted. But when we let go of all that and come back to zero point, then what appeared to be constricting and constraining transmutes into something that is quite open and wide.

To reach that point, we must relate to ourselves and our life situations and our experiences as opportunities. Jon Kabat-Zinn wrote a book, *Wherever You Go, There You Are*,[5] making that point. Many times we think about changing our situation, or changing our circumstances, or going somewhere else, or being something else, or doing something else. But when you completely accept yourself as you are and use your circumstances as the field of practice, then having no choice will become *big* choice. That is passing through the net.

Of course, when you pass through the net, then you perceive another kind of net. When you leave this tight, personalized, self-enclosed, constructed net of your own making, you perceive a universal net of interconnectedness, where each one of us is a juncture point or knot in the webbing of the net. In this net we are all supporting one another. The knot that I am over here supports the knot that you are over there.

There is a saying in Buddhism: "On the ceiling of heaven the god Indra makes a net." And at each juncture point—at each knot of the net—there is a jewel. That jewel reflects each and every other jewel in the net as well as the totality of the net. So there is reflection, reflection, reflection going on perpetually. Not only do we support one another and reflect one another in this universal perception of "internettedness," but in some mysterious way, each of us is also the complete net. Think of it this way: In a series of numbers from 1 to 10, each number is the whole series. It is absurd to talk about a series of numbers from 1 to 10 without having 1; so 1 makes the whole series. You cannot have a series of numbers from 1 to 10 without 4; so 4, likewise, is the whole series. And you cannot have a series of numbers from 1 to 10 without 9; so 9 makes the whole series.

In some way we are all supporting one another. And simultaneously, we are in some way the essence of the whole universal structure of everything. If you get a glimpse of this, then you begin to see where compassionate activity arises, you begin to see where a real, grounded sense of responsibility arises, and you begin to enter into a sense of community.

The fish that has passed through the net: If you are relating to the world in that way, then, of course, each and every experience becomes nourishment. The Chinese Zen master Lin-chi (Jap., Rinzai) said, "Your true teacher is always just before you." This means that all experience becomes your teacher. That is why the third great vow of the bodhisattva path says, "The teachings are infinite; I vow to learn them all." If I can value each experience as it is, then each experience becomes a valuable teaching interaction.

Maezumi Roshi, the Japanese Zen master who started the Los Angeles Zen Center, would often emphasize this point—that we should appreciate all aspects of our life. This doesn't mean we should appreciate everything in some aesthetic way. You can look at the blue sky with the white clouds floating and feel, "Ahhhh, blue sky, that's wonderful." Or you can look at the red flower in the garden and get transfixed and feel, "Ohhhh, wonderful!" But if you perceive starvation and suffering and injustice and inhumanity, you cannot appreciate it as, "Ahhhh, wonderful." So, to appreciate the experiences of our life is not just to turn the whole world into some huge art gallery. If you see suffering, then you are moved to sadness; if you see injustice, you are moved to righteous indignation. Those experiences are the energy out of which compassionate activity may arise. To appreciate all aspects of our life is to be able to see the usefulness in the feelings and experiences that we have.

There is, however, also a potential pitfall in appreciating everything and seeing it all as food and nourishment: The world may look too dazzling and enticing and exciting. The mandala of creative activity may be too bright at that time. You have not come fully to the Zen of the old cow or the floppy old dog. This means that as practice becomes mature, it becomes absolutely ordinary, like an old cow eating grass or a floppy old dog. One could say almost boring.

Think about Zen illustrations, not just of the Buddha, but of monks and nuns. In most statues, the Buddha is sitting majestically—erect, open, and serene. The image is inspiring. But if you look at Zen pictures of an old monk or nun sitting in meditation, you may see that they are not sitting so majestically; sometimes they are sitting with kind of a crooked back, and are looking up at the moon. That is the Zen of the "complete flop." All the dazzle, all the appreciation and the glitter has fallen away. That means that everyone—even Buddha in his great enlightenment—still has to get up in the morning and brush his or her teeth, and still has to go to sleep at night. That is the last word of Zen—the complete flop, the old cow or floppy old dog.

Dogen Zenji, the great Japanese Zen master who founded the Soto Zen sect in Japan, was asked what he had attained by going to China. He said, "The eyes are horizontal, the nose is vertical." That is all, just, "The eyes are horizontal, the nose is vertical." There's nothing special there, it's very plain but also universal. In the Japanese Nichiren tradition, where they chant the mantra, "*Namu Myoho Renge Kyo*," there is a teaching that says, "The Buddha is still sitting on Vulture Peak, perpetually teaching the *Lotus Sutra*." That means we can all go there, even now, and see the Buddha face-to-face. Now seeing the Buddha face-to-face sounds very special and extraordinary.

Have you seen the Buddha face-to-face? In response to this question, you might—like the monks in Man Gong's assembly—shout "KATZ!" Or you might hit the floor. Or you might raise a fist. Or you might say, "The sky is blue, the tree is green." All that, of course, is seeing the Buddha face-to-face. However, the old Zen masters might say that all of these responses still have the stink of Zen about them. But if you come completely around the circle—start at $0°$ and come all the way around to $360°$—then you can only say, "The eyes are horizontal, the nose is vertical."

I hope that we all attain, "The eyes are horizontal, the nose is vertical," and help this world in some way.

ZEN MASTER KO BONG'S "DIAMOND PARAMITA"

If seeing and hearing are clear, then you understand
your original gifts and can allow them to flow
freely into the world.

If seeing and hearing are not clear, then you have to
relinquish the eyes and ears, sights and sounds,
image and concept of the one who sees and hears.

Hanging off the edge of a cliff, let go and fall ten
thousand feet just in a second and vividly come to
life.

Do you perceive the point of this or not?

. . . . .

Six divided by six equals one.

Zen Master Ko Bong, who lived from 1890 to 1962, used his "Diamond Paramita" kong-an as a tool to teach about the *paramitas* (the virtues perfected by the bodhisattva). Zen Master Tachu, who was a successor of Zen Master Ma-tsu (Jap., Baso; Kor., Ma Jo), also offered important teachings on the *paramitas*. Between them, their stories offer a look at modern Korean Zen and its origin in ancient China.

Zen Master Ko Bong, considered one of the greatest teachers

of his time in Korea, was the most prominent of Zen Master Man Gong's twenty-five dharma successors. However, before becoming a monk and then a Zen master, the young Ko Bong was seen as rather arrogant. Sometimes he would stand in front of a temple and shout, "Somebody come here and cut my hair! I want to become a monk." The temple's monks would become angry and threaten to beat him, but he would just taunt them: "You can hit my body, but you cannot hit my mind. If you hit my mind, I will become your disciple."

One day Zen Master Hae Bong heard this and came out. He asked Ko Bong, "How many pounds does your mind weigh?" At that, Ko Bong felt stuck and could not answer, so he cut his own hair and became a monk.

Several years later, while still a student, Ko Bong had a major breakthrough. During a summer retreat at Tongdosa Temple, he was sitting meditation on some rocks under a big tree. While courageously keeping don't-know mind one hundred percent, he heard a cicada singing in the tree above him. His mind opened and he got enlightenment. Filled with jubilation, he spontaneously hit the rocks with his fan, breaking it. "That's it!" he exclaimed and laughed uncontrollably.

It is worth noting here that *kaech'im*, "broken," is one of the Korean words used for enlightenment. The connotation is that the small egocentric *I* breaks open as one experiences a breakthrough to truth as it is. Later, as a Zen master, Ko Bong would sometimes test students with a kong-an that relates to this process:

> The mouse eats cat food, but the cat bowl is broken.
> What does this mean?

In spite of his prominence, many still considered Ko Bong's behavior unorthodox. As a Zen master he was renowned for refusing to teach monks, considering them too lazy and arrogant to become good Zen students. So he taught mainly nuns and laypeople.

Once, taking the high seat, Zen Master Ko Bong held up his Zen stick and said:

> Inside it is bright.
> Outside it is also bright.
> Wherever it is, it is bright.
> What is it?

Everyone was silent. "That is the 'Diamond Paramita,'" he said, then laid down his Zen stick.[1]

Now, let's look at Tachu. When he first came to call on Zen Master Ma-tsu, Ma-tsu asked, "Where are you coming from?" That means, "At this very moment, seeing, hearing, even your sense of *I*-ness, all emerge from where? At this very moment, seeing and hearing are an expression of what?"

But Tachu said, "I have come from Ta-yun Monastery in Yueh Chou."

Then Ma-tsu asked him, "What is your intention in coming here?" [*You might also ask, "What is my intention just now? Why read a book on Zen or sit in meditation? Why follow the Zen way? What is the intention or direction of this?"*]

Tachu said, "I have come here to seek the Buddha-dharma." At that point, you could say that Ma-tsu had completely sized up Tachu and seen through him. What Tachu needed had become exposed.

Ma-tsu then asked, "Without looking at your own treasure, for what purpose are you leaving your home and walking around? Here I do not have a single thing. What Buddha-dharma are you looking for?"

That must have been quite disappointing for Tachu, who had

just made a long journey to seek the Buddha-dharma, for in that last sentence Mat-tsu cut the legs out from under him. Tachu replied, "What, then, is my own treasure?"

Here his investigation becomes clearer and much more intimate. Ma-tsu said, "That which is asking me right now is your own treasure, perfectly complete; it lacks nothing. You are free to use it. Why are you seeking outside?" Upon hearing this, Tachu realized the original mind, which does not rely on knowledge or understanding. Overjoyed, he paid his respects to the patriarch and thanked him. After that he stayed with Ma-tsu for six years, serving as his disciple. This point is worth noting: Even after having some insight, he stayed for six years to study and refine what he had perceived in that moment.

Later Tachu returned to Yueh Chou and composed a treatise entitled *Discourse on the Essentials of Entering the Way through Sudden Awakening*.[2] When Ma-tsu saw the text, he said to the assembly, "In Yueh Chou there is a great pearl named Tachu. Its perfect brilliance shines freely without obstruction."

In Tachu's treatise, written in the form of questions and answers, a questioner asks Tachu, "By what means can the gateway of our school be entered?"

Tachu answers, "By means of *dana-paramita* [the *paramita*, or perfection, of giving]."

The questioner then says, "According to the Buddha, the Bodhisattva Path comprises six *paramitas*. Why then have you mentioned only one? Please explain why this one alone provides sufficient means for us to enter."

Before going further, I need to say a bit more about the meaning of *paramita* and explain the traditional view of the six *paramitas*. *Paramita* literally means "to cross over" and has the connotation of "to transcend." As I have noted, these *paramitas* are also referred to as the six perfections, and *perfection* is a second, common translation of *paramita*. In the bodhisattva path of Mahayana Buddhism and of Zen, the *paramitas* are practices that point toward altruistic activity. The word *perfection* here does not mean some kind of idealized trip that you go on as you try to become perfect. The *paramitas* include the *prajna-paramita* that we chant about in the *Heart Sutra*. *Prajna-paramita* means the perfection of wisdom. But if you say, "I have attained the perfection of wisdom," at that moment you have attained the perfection of ignorance. And if you say, "I have attained the perfection of generosity," at that moment you are quite far from perfecting generosity. As soon as you reflect and say, "I have attained this," you miss the essential point. So the word *perfection* here has the connotation of an ongoing practice of refinement.

At this point, I'd like to return to Zen Master Ko Bong's kong-an:

> Inside it is bright.
> Outside it is also bright.
> Wherever it is, it is bright.
> What is it?

When commenting on this kong-an, he said:

> When gold is in the ground, it is bright. If you put gold into a hot furnace, it is bright. After being in the furnace, gold is still bright. Before it went through the furnace it could not be made to make anything. Also, when in the furnace it cannot be used. But after it comes out of the furnace, we can use it to make many things: a ring, earrings or a hair pin. What is the furnace [where the gold is refined]? The furnace is the *paramitas*, giving, morality, patience, practices, meditation and wisdom.[3]

Dana-paramita (giving or generosity) implies the practice of compassionate activity. This means that everything that I have and everything that I am is not only for me but for all beings. It means helping in both a material sense and in a teaching sense. Zen Master Ko Bong, when he commented on the first *paramita*, said, "Forget these three things—*I, you, give*—then you are practicing the generosity *paramita.*"

The second, called the *shila-paramita*, is sometimes translated as practicing the precepts, or the practicing of morality. Keeping the precepts is usually understood to mean that you purify yourself by practicing these disciplines, but this is not the Zen understanding. Think about it this way: If you had hidden some Jews from the Nazis in Germany, when the SS knocked on your door and asked if you had seen any Jews, you would have kept your precept of truthfulness by replying, "Yes, there are some hiding in the attic." But you would have missed the true and essential spirit of the precept. The Zen perspective on precepts is encapsulated in the following sentence: "Know when the precepts are open and when they are closed. Know when to keep them and when to break them."[4] This is the essential bodhisattva spirit of the precepts. Ko Bong, commenting on morality, said, "Whether giving or receiving only do what is correct, then good and bad become clear. Then your clear action will 'kill' good and bad. But, do not attach to good and bad. This is the morality *paramita.*"[5]

There is a famous story about Ko Bong giving the Five Precepts to layperson Chung Dong Go Sanim. The ceremony was going smoothly until the section where the preceptor recites the precepts and asks, "Can these precepts be kept by you or not?"

Suddenly the layman stood up and said, "If I cannot drink I die!" Now, there was a problem.

But Ko Bong responded immediately, "Then you take only

four precepts." Chung Dong Go Sanim became the "Four Pre-cepts Layman," and got "four precepts enlightenment."[6]

The *kshanti-paramita* translates as patience, endurance, or perseverance. In one sense, the practice of patience is rooted in an insight that all problems and difficulties have causes. Thus when you are enduring something difficult, you may have some insight into the fact that some set of causes has led up to it, and therefore have some understanding of karma. Sometimes when I am experiencing something I do not like very much, I will say jokingly to my wife, "I must have done something terrible in my last life." But whether or not you believe in previous lives, some sense of causality is there. If you accept that, then on some level you are accepting the responsibility for where you are and what you intend to do about the difficult situation in which you find yourself.

When discussing this patience *paramita*, Ko Bong Sunim said, "If something is bothering you, be patient and forgiving. A pa-tient mind will make you happy; then inside you will feel pride and want to try harder. This is the patience *paramita*."[7] When he says, "If you are patient then you will feel pride," he makes an interesting point. Usually when people think about spiritual practices, they think about cultivating humility and eradicating pride. But here he says the opposite. "Pride," he explains, "is like a pond plant that has no roots—it comes and goes freely." This means the phenomenon of feeling pride just as it is, with-out doing anything about it, floats freely. It arises and it passes on. The energy of that is enlivening. He says, "Fear only that you will fall into indulgence." If you do not let pride float freely, but instead grasp it tightly and connect too much *I*-ness to it, then it becomes an obstacle. But pride in itself is just an energy we can use like anything else.

The fourth, fifth, and sixth *paramitas* go together. The fourth, *virya-paramita*, is translated as effort or energy, the practice of zeal and exertion. It is connected with the attitude of sincere trying. The bodhisattva practices include the Great Vow: "Sentient beings are numberless, I vow to save them all." Zen Master Seung Sahn used to express it with a short aphorism, "Try, try, try, for ten thousand years nonstop." Trying sincerely also requires the willingness to be open. This is keeping the Great Vow, having great energy and attention. It means that at any moment, regardless of whether you feel good or you feel bad, or the situation is good or bad, you only try to help others. That is the energy *paramita*, sometimes translated as the *practice paramita*. To practice these things requires the kind of intention that is ongoing. If you lose that intention, you have to rearouse it over and over again.

When Ko Bong was a young monk, he was not particularly interested in chanting practice and learning the forms of the ceremonies where Buddhist monks sometimes officiate. He only did sitting meditation practice. Once, when he was staying at a small hilltop temple, the abbot left him in charge. One morning an old woman climbed the steep road to the temple carrying fruit and a bag of rice on her back, and found Ko Bong meditating alone in the Buddha Hall. She apologized for disturbing him and asked for his help, saying, "My family is having a lot of problems. I would like someone to chant to the Buddha for them."

Ko Bong looked her in the eye and perceived her sincerity and sadness, and replied, "No problem. I'd be happy to chant for you." They went to the kitchen to prepare the food offering. As they started to wash the fruit, Ko Bong said, "If you cook the rice, I will go and begin the chanting." Ko Bong put on his ceremonial robes even though he had never learned the appropriate Buddhist chants. He dug out a Taoist sutra from among his things and took it to the Buddha Hall. Then he picked up the wooden drum in the shape of a fish, used for chanting, and began to hit it while chanting from the Taoist text. After an hour or so, when he had finished, the old woman thanked him for his kindness, saying that she now felt much better.

As she was walking down the hill to her village, the old woman met the abbot on his way back to the temple. She told the abbot about her family troubles and how Ko Bong had helped her. The abbot looked confused and said to her, "Ko Bong Sunim doesn't know how to do any chanting." The woman replied, "No, no, he did very well; he helped me a lot."

Actually, the old woman had known that Ko Bong was chanting from a Taoist text because she had once been a nun and was therefore familiar with the real chanting service for the occasion. She said to the abbot, "He did very well. He chanted one hundred percent! The words are not important. The only thing is how you keep your mind. Ko Bong Sunim had only try mind—only just do it."

Later, when the abbot saw Ko Bong, he said to him, "You chanted for Mrs. Lee, but you don't know anything about chanting." Ko Bong answered, "That's right, I don't know anything about chanting, so I just chanted."

Fifth is the *dhyana-paramita*, meditation. This means keeping a mind that is not moving in any situation or condition. Your mind is like a mirror: If red comes, it reflects red; if white comes, it reflects white. The mirror itself never loses its integrity as a mirror regardless of what it is reflecting. The practice of meditation is: Moment by moment, what are you doing just now? It is very simple; there is no need to make it complicated. "Moment by moment, what are you doing just now?" also means that meditation practice is not just for use on the cushion in the dharma room. If meditation practice were just for that, then this practice would not connect with everyday life; it would be a lopsided kind of spirituality. If you think that meditation is very special, it then becomes an obstacle or hindrance to practice. On the other hand, this does not mean that formal meditation practice is unnecessary. If you think, "I don't need to sit in formal meditation because I'm trying moment by moment to see what I am doing just now," you are also fooling yourself. Ko Bong Sunim said: "Meditation is originally nothing special. Just keep a strong practice mind. If you want to get rid of distractions and get enlightenment, this is a mistake. Throw away this kind of thinking; only keep a strong mind and practice. Then you will gradually enter 'just do it.'[8]

"Everyone wants to understand meditation, but they think about it in terms of medicine and disease. However, don't be afraid of what you *think* of as a disease. Only be afraid of going too slow, of not making a strong, consistent, concerted effort. Some day you will get enlightenment."

At the Providence Zen Center we had a discussion recently about the quality of generosity in practice. Zen Master Soeng Hyang (Barbara Rhodes) was there and commented, "A couple of times in my life I've been very fortunate to be able to go on a retreat all alone for a hundred days. It was during those retreats that I had some experience where I perceived spontaneously what some of these things mean—things like generosity, zeal, meditation, etc. I encourage everyone to go on a hundred-day retreat." Of course, not everyone is able to do this, although sometimes we think it is impossible to go on a retreat like this when it really is not. Still—whether you go on a hundred-day, week-long, or three-day retreat—it is important that you remove yourself from your complex life from time to time in order to practice in an intensive way. In a simple setting you can get an intuitive sense of what some of these teachings are truly about. This is an important aspect of Zen training.

The sixth *paramita* is the *prajna-paramita,* the wisdom *paramita.* It tells us that when our practice becomes digested and assimilated, then clear seeing and clear acting, according to our situation moment by moment, becomes possible. Our mind becomes pure and clear. This is sometimes referred to as *everyday Zen* or *last word Zen.* Ko Bong Sunim said:

> If something comes, do not be happy. If something goes, do not be sad. When you cry, just cry. When you laugh, just laugh. Things are created, linger, decline and empty. Feelings change from happy to sad, joy to anger. Countries arise and prosper and then they decline and are destroyed. If you perceive this without attaching to it, this is the wisdom *paramita.*[9]

Those are the six *paramitas* from a traditional point of view. In Tachu's treatise, the student asks, "What is the gateway to our school?"

To which Tachu replies, "It is the *dana-paramita.*"

The student asks, "Why, when there are these six, do you only put emphasis on this one?"

Tachu responds, "Deluded people fail to understand that the other five all proceed from the *dana-paramita,* and by its practice, all the others are fulfilled." Further along in the treatise, he says, "We give different names to these six methods only for convenience in dealing with passing needs. But when we come to the marvelous principle involved in them all, we find no differences at all." In his book *Zen Mind, Beginner's Mind,* Suzuki Roshi says something similar: "Actually these 'prajna paramitas' are one, but as we can observe life from various sides, we count six."[10]

The next part of the treatise asks, "Why is it called *dana-paramita?*" and Tachu replies, "*Dana* means relinquishment." This is interesting, because ordinarily it is translated as *giving* or *generosity*. Relinquishment has the connotation of giving up something, letting go of or surrendering something. In Buddhist terminology it connotes the practice and view of nonattachment.

The student then asks, "Relinquishment of what?"

Tachu answers, "Relinquishment of the dualism of opposites. Let go of all ideas of good and bad, being and not being, love and aversion, empty and not empty, pure and impure, concentration and distraction—let go of all of it."

That last one, distraction, is important for formal meditation practice and relates to Ko Bong's statements. Many times students will say, "When I sit, I think my mind is distracted or daydreaming about ninety-five percent of the time and five percent of the time I have concentration." Here Tachu says, let go of looking at your mind in that dualistic way. Do not compare concentration with distraction. Consider the metaphor of the blue sky with the bright sun shining while clouds are passing back and forth. Sometimes you see the blue sky and bright sun clearly, at other times you do not see them, because clouds are passing back and forth. But essentially, even the clouds are part of the blue sky. They are not separate from it. When you sit in meditation, have an essential recognition that your distracting thoughts and original, clear mind are not two. If you can sit with that kind of confidence in the not-twoness of all of that, then you are not disturbed by your "distracting thoughts." You will then settle down and become open and clearly perceptive. That is the view of the *dana-paramita* as relinquishment.

In his discussion of this, Suzuki Roshi says, "To give is to be non-attached. To not attach is to give."[11] The first statement is clear—if I give you my Zen stick, then I am not attached to it. But to be nonattached is *to give*? That is not so logically clear. It means that originally we have the innate quality of generosity. If we are not clinging and reducing ourselves to some small, grasping, egoistic perception, then generosity is already there; we are one with the world we are embedded in. Tachu says, "Our self-nature does not contain a single thing foreign to itself." The ten thousand things, all phenomena that we encounter in this world, are myself. What you see is yourself. What you hear is yourself. What you experience is yourself. This means that your original self is quite large and that largeness is the innate quality of generosity. When you perceive that original oneness, you see that you are already giving everything. Everything in nature is already giving—the sun is continuously giving, the rain and wind are continuously giving, the four elements are continuously giving to us. Likewise, we also have that quality.

I remember many years ago when I was a music student in a conservatory, I walked into the concert hall, where a pianist was rehearsing. He was playing quite well, but at that time I tended to be critical of everybody and everything. I started thinking, probably motivated by my envy of how well he was playing, "His technique is a little shoddy, his phrasing could be a little better." I had begun to study Eastern philosophy by that time, and I suddenly asked myself, "Why can't you just feel that you're playing through him?" When I had that reminder, all the criticalness—*ptchh*—dropped away for the time being and I just appreciated his music as an expression of giving—he was giving, I was giving, everybody was giving.

There is one more point connected with this: Whenever we give something, essentially it is never really coming from our egoistic, small *I*. When something is given, it turns us back to the question, "Who is the one who is doing this act of giving?" That don't-know mind *is* the mind of generosity and openness. Ko Bong says, "When giving, forget these three things—*I*, *you* and *give*."[12] Then, at that moment, there is just one complete action. That action is don't-know action, generosity in its pure form. That is our innate quality.

Another student, who was at the discussion about generosity that I referred to, told a story about her father, who has cancer. He has been getting progressively worse over the last couple of years, but is—and always has been—an extremely independent person. Although the family thought he should go into a nursing home, he flatly refused. Then the family suggested that if he was going to stay at home, personal care attendants should be coming in. Again, he refused. It became a big problem, especially when he would fall because of his weakened state. His wife was unable to pick him up, because she, too, was not so strong anymore. Recently, however, things had changed. He had gone to the hospital again. When the student who was recounting this story went to visit him shortly before he was released, he said to her, "I think it's time to bring in some help when I go back home." She said that in his relinquishment of independence, he was generously giving to everybody else concerned. She said, "I felt it was a great gift to me. My mother thought it was a great gift to her." Sometimes relinquishment and generosity happen just like that.

In the Japanese Zen tradition there is a story where all these *paramitas* come together. There was a monk named Tetsugen, who lived several hundred years ago. He wanted to have a printing of the Buddhist canon done in vernacular Japanese so that the common people could read it. At that time the sutras were written only in Chinese characters. Tetsugen started traveling all around Japan, begging money for the printing. It took him about ten years to collect enough to hire someone to make the wood blocks for the printing. Just when he was about to hire the person, there was a big flood. Many people lost their homes and no one knew what they were going to do. Tetsugen took the money he had collected for the sutras and helped people rebuild their homes. After that, he started traveling again, begging money to print the sutras. Again he traveled for close to ten years, collected enough money, and was just about to hire somebody to carve the wood blocks when there was an intense drought. The rice crop was spoiled and there was no food. Once more, Tetsugen spent the money, this time purchasing rice for people who had no food. After he had taken care of them, he started out again on foot and begged money for the sutras. The third time he actually got the sutras printed. The Japanese people said, "The monk Tetsugen did three printings of the sutras, but of these three the first two were much better than the last."

There is one more relinquishment story that I am fond of. A student came to call on Zen Master Hyang Bong and said, "Please, master, teach me the Dharma."

Hyang Bong said, "I'm sorry, but my Dharma is very expensive."

"Oh, then how much does it cost?" asked the student.

"How much can you pay?" was Hyang Bong's answer.

The student put his hand in his pocket and took out some coins and told him, "This is all the money I have."

Hyang Bong said, "Even if you offered me a pile of gold as big as a mountain, my Dharma would still be more expensive."

The student went off and started practicing. After a few months of hard training, he returned to Hyang Bong and said, "Master I will give you my life. I will do anything for you. I will be your slave. Please teach me your Dharma."

Hyang Bong replied, "Even if you offered me a thousand lives, my Dharma is still too expensive."

The student was quite dejected. He went off and practiced diligently for several months more. Then he came back and said, "Master I will give you my mind. Will you teach me now?"

Hyang Bong said, "Your mind is a pail of stinking garbage. I have no use for it. Even if you offered me ten thousand minds, my Dharma would still be too expensive."

Again the student left to do very hard training, and after some time he came to an understanding that the whole universe is empty. So he returned to the master and said, "Now I understand how expensive your Dharma is."

Hyang Bong then asked, "Well, how expensive is it?"

The student shouted, "KATZ!"

Hyang Bong said, "No, it's more expensive than that."

This time the student was thoroughly confused and in deep despair. He vowed not to see the master again until he had achieved a supreme awakening.

Eventually that day came, and he returned. He said, "Master, now I truly understand—the sky is blue, the grass is green."

Hyang Bong answered, "My Dharma is even more expensive than that."

At this point the student got furious and said, "I already understand. I don't need your Dharma. You can take it and shove it up your ass!"

Hyang Bong laughed, which made the student even angrier. He wheeled around and started to stomp out of the room. Just as he was about to go out the door, Hyang Bong called to him, "Wait a minute!" The student turned his head and Hyang Bong said, "Don't lose my Dharma."

Zen Master Ko Bong said:

The sun is in the sky whether it is clear or cloudy. Gold is gold whether it is in the ground, in the furnace or in your hand. The "Diamond Paramita" is just like that—not dependent on life or death, coming or going, or time and space. If you can see it, I will hit you thirty times. If you cannot see it, I will also hit you thirty times. What can you do?

$6 \times 6 = 36$[13]

Then he got down from the high seat.

ZEN MASTER SEUNG SAHN'S "DROPPING ASHES ON THE BUDDHA"

Understanding that all things are one;
Do you also understand that the ten thousand things
*   forever remain distinct?*
If you fall down in emptiness, you may lose your life.
No point giving medicine to a dead horse.
Become one,
Distinctness, clinging to nothingness.
What is it that transcends these?
Look!
Above blue sky,
In front of the door green trees,
Below your feet the brown wooden floor.

During the early days of Zen in China, there was one master who was fond of using this teaching phrase: "The whole world in the ten directions is one bright jewel."

One day a monk came forward in the assembly and said, "Master, you always say the whole world in the ten directions is one bright jewel. How is one to understand that?"

The Zen master responded, "This whole world in the ten directions is one bright jewel. What has understanding got to do with it?"

The next day, when the master was walking around the grounds of the temple, he saw the monk and said to him, "This whole world in the ten directions is one bright jewel. How do you understand that?"

The monk replied, "This whole world in the ten directions is one bright jewel. What has understanding got to do with it?"

The Zen master said, "I knew you were making your living in a ghost cave on the far side of the mountain," and walked away.

Seen from a certain perspective, this is a story about flexibility. One time, "What has understanding got to do with it?" The other time, "How do you understand that?" All the while holding to this one point, "The whole world in the ten directions is one bright jewel."

Flexibility means free functioning. How can we perceive something in this moment, yet let go of it in the very next moment? How can we perceive something from one perspective, then from another perspective a moment later? How can we sometimes see something from two perspectives simultaneously? And most important, how can we use that clear seeing to function freely and help this world?

Zen Master Seung Sahn has one kong-an that he uses to test students, called "Dropping Ashes on the Buddha." This kong-an emphasizes the different aspects of Zen seeing and functioning. But before going into the kong-an, let me say a little about my teacher. Seung Sahn Dae Soen Sa Nim (*Soen Sa Nim* is Korean for *Zen Master*; *Dae* means *great* or *complete*, and is a title given to older, respected teachers) was born in 1927 and is the dharma successor to Zen Master Ko Bong. After the end of the Second

World War, when he was in his late teens and feeling that his academic studies were not satisfying his deeper questions, Seung Sahn became a novice monk. Shortly thereafter he went to Won Gak Mountain to do a hundred-day solo retreat during which he chanted the "Great Dharani of the Mystic Mind Energy," a long mantra associated with the bodhisattva of universal compassion. Near the end of the retreat, he had a deep awakening and wrote this enlightenment poem:

> The road at the bottom of Won Gak Mountain
> Is not the present road.
> The Man climbing the hill with his backpack
> Is not a man of the past.
>
> Tok, tok—his footsteps
> Transfix past and present.
>
> Crows out of a tree.
> Caw, caw, caw.[1]

When Seung Sahn descended from the mountain, he joined a small Zen community of laypeople at Magoksa Temple. There, in 1949, he met Zen Master Ko Bong, who asked him the kong-an:

> Why did Bodhidharma come to China?
> Joju [Chin., Chao-chou; Jap., Joshu] answered, "The
>   cyprus tree in the garden."
> What does this mean?

Seung Sahn understood, but because he was new to Zen, he did not know how to respond. He replied, "I don't know."

"Only keep this don't-know mind," said Ko Bong. "This is true Zen practice."

In the fall of the same year, Seung Sahn went to Sudoksa

Temple to sit the three-month winter retreat. There he heard monks and Zen masters engage each other in dharma combat and began to master the style of Zen language. When the retreat ended he went to Seoul to see Ko Bong again. On the way, he had interviews with Zen Masters Keum Bong and Keum Oh. In their dharma combat with Seung Sahn, each acknowledged his awakening. When he again met Ko Bong, they had an intense interview during which Seung Sahn was stuck for a while, for Ko Bong refused to accept answers to the kong-an he had posed. The two sat facing each other in tense silence for fifty minutes, then suddenly the correct answer appeared to Seung Sahn, and Ko Bong said, "Your flower has blossomed and I am the bee."

In 1950 Seung Sahn received dharma transmission from Ko Bong, making him the seventy-eighth patriarch in that particular line from Shakyamuni Buddha. Ko Bong said, "Some day Korean Buddhism will spread to the whole world through you. We will meet again in five hundred years."

Seung Sahn spent the next three years in silence to deepen his experience and understanding. After the Korean War, during which he served as a chaplain in the army, he became abbot of Hwagyesa Temple in Seoul. He also looked after his aging and sick teacher Ko Bong. He was the visiting Zen master of five temples in Seoul and the instructor in Zen at Dongguk University.

An interesting episode from this period concerns the bones of five hundred dead kept in what had been a Japanese temple in Seoul, which was now under the control of some Korean laypeople. At that time there was still considerable bad feeling toward the Japanese. The people in charge of the temple wanted to throw away the bones of their former enemies. When Zen Master Seung Sahn heard of this, he had the bones removed to Hwagyesa Temple, where he chanted the rite for the dead spirits for days on end. He proclaimed: "Whether these bones were once Korean or Japanese is immaterial. Dead bones are dead bones!" A few years later, when Korea and Japan resumed diplomatic relations, some Japanese came to Hwagyesa and carried the bones of their ancestors back to their homeland. Out of appreciation and deep respect for Seung Sahn's action, the Japanese invited him to go to Japan. Thus, during the 1960s, he also taught in Japan, as well as in Hong Kong.

In 1972 Seung Sahn decided to come to the United Sates to teach. After spending a short time in Los Angeles, he went to Providence, Rhode Island. He had almost no money and knew only a few words of English. He took a job repairing washing machines in a Korean-run laundromat, then rented an apartment—meanwhile taking a course in English at Harvard University. Soon some students from Brown University began coming to study with him, and the Providence Zen Center was born.

Within the next few years, Zen centers in Cambridge, New Haven, New York, Berkeley, and Los Angeles began to form around his teaching and under his guidance. Later Seung Sahn went to Poland and other eastern and western European countries, where more centers were formed and evolved. Eventually, all the meditation centers became part of the Kwan Um School of Zen. By then he had fulfilled Ko Bong's prophesy that Korean Buddhism would "spread to the whole world through you."

In the years that followed, Seung Sahn's kong-an, "Dropping Ashes on the Buddha," became a major teaching tool. It says:

> Someone comes into the Zen center, blows smoke, and drops ashes on the Buddha. It you are there at that time, how can you fix this person's mind?[2]

The first question, of course, is, "Who is this person who comes into the Zen Center, blows smoke, and drops ashes on the Buddha?" Well, surprise, surprise! From one perspective, it is none other than ourselves. How are we making a big smokescreen and obscuring what actually is? How are we covering things with our own conceptions, opinions, and ideation? How are we dropping ashes on the Buddha and covering it with dust?

This kong-an also poses some other questions, for instance, "What is the Zen Center? Is it this room? Is it some particular place?" And, "Is there *coming into* or *going out of* something called the Zen Center?" If you think there is coming into and going out of the Zen Center, you have missed the original Zen Center. But, on the other hand, if you think that there is a Zen Center apart from coming into and going out of, that is also not seeing clearly. Form is emptiness; emptiness is, itself, form.

I was reminded of this the other day when I received a catalogue from Sonoma Mountain Zen Center, in California, which is led by Jakusho Kwong Roshi, a successor of Suzuki Roshi. They sell such things as incense, meditation beads, Buddha statues, books, and tapes in their store. The title of the catalogue was *Zen Dust*. Once I went to the New Haven Zen Center and found a rack with incoming and outgoing mail. They had one shelf holding flyers from every meditation center in the universe. They had labeled it "Dharma Junk. If you want something, take."

From the most fundamental, radical perspective, of course, many things—the incense, the gold Buddha, the beads—even these chapters—are junk, or "dust." But sometimes dust is quite useful; it depends how you use it.

In the classical kong-ans of *The Blue Cliff Record*, there are two cases that make similar points to the "Dropping Ashes" kong-an. One is called "Mu-chou's Impostor":

One day a monk approached Zen master Mu-chou (Jap., Bokushu; Kor., Muk Ju), and Mu-chou asked, "Just now, where are you coming from?"

The monk shouted, "KATZ!"

Mu-chou said, "You shouted at this old monk once." [*That means, "Your shout is not bad as a first response, a demonstration of the nameless energy that everything emerges from, but is that all? Or is there something else that you have to present?"*]

The monk shouted a second time.

Mu-chou said, "And after four or five shouts, then what?"

The monk was speechless, so Mu-chou hit him and said, "You impostor!"[3]

Where are *you* coming from just now? Moment by moment, coming from where? From one perspective, everything comes from this unnamable, ungraspable, inconceivable point. But if you are attached to that, then you become completely blind. That is why Mu-chou said, "After four or five shouts, then what?"

A second related case is a story about Dok Sahn (Chin., Te-shan; Jap., Tokusan) and Wi Sahn (Chin.. Kuei-shan; Jap., Isan). When Dok Sahn was a young monk, he was very fiery. He had had some kind of breakthrough experience and had a lot of fire in his belly from this experience, presenting himself fiercely and radically. Eventually he got a reputation as that kind of fellow. He came to have an interview with Zen Master Wi Sahn and, the story says, "He came into the dharma room still carrying his bundle."

When monks at that time traveled the roads from one temple to another, they would keep their ceremonial dress in something like a knapsack. When they got to a temple, they would take off their dusty road-traveling clothes and put on their ceremonial monks' clothes before going into a dharma hall or meeting the Zen master. But here it says that Dok Sahn came into the dharma room "still carrying his bundle." It is a telling expression. Carrying what? Holding on to what?

> Then he walked from east to west and west to east, across the room, and said, "There is nothing, nothing."

Nothing, in Chinese, is the word *wu* (Kor. & Jap., *mu*). After "Nothing, nothing," the compiler of these stories—they probably existed for a few hundred years before being turned into anthologies—wrote a comment, almost a little heckle: "Completely exposed." Then the story continues:

> And [Dok Sahn] walked out. But when he got to the gate, he thought to himself, "I should not be so brash." So he composed himself, put down his bundle for a moment, and came back into the dharma room and did a prostration. But then he held up his sitting mat and yelled out, "Master!" Wi Sahn grabbed for his horsehair whisk and held it up. [*In those days, the Zen master would have had a horsehair whisk as a symbol saying, "I am the Zen master."*] Then, Dok Sahn suddenly shouted, "KATZ!" whirled around, and walked out of the dharma hall. He put on his straw sandals and left.

The compiler writes in again, "Completely exposed." The story continues:

> That night Wi Sahn asked the head monk, "That newcomer who was here this morning, what happened to him?"

The head monk said, "When he got to the door, he put on his straw sandals and never turned back."

Wi Sahn said, "Some day that fellow will go to a high summit, build himself a small hut, and go on cursing the Buddhas and the patriarchs."

After that, the compiler writes, "Adding frost to snow"[4]— redundant.

If you look at the person in the "Dropping Ashes" kong-an, you see a similar position: What is completely exposed there?

In one way you have to admire that person. There is a certain tenacity, really holding to a position and not letting go. As Zen Master Seung Sahn says, "This man is very strong. To any speech or action of yours, he will only hit you. This man thinks, 'I already have enlightenment. I already am Buddha.'" No life, no death—he has attained one point. But he is attached to his one point, attached to emptiness.

However, tenacity can turn into rigidity when you are afraid to let go and face creative uncertainty, and that becomes a problem. What is Dok Sahn afraid to let go of? His *nothing*. It has become his prized possession. "Nothing, nothing! KATZ!" And what is the cigarette man, the man blowing smoke and dropping ashes on the Buddha, afraid of letting go of? His view of oneness, that all things are one and empty of name and form: cigarettes, ashes, Buddha, they are all the same for him.

Once an eminent Zen master, addressing the assembly, posed a question: "[The mind is] like a mirror casting images. When an image is formed, where has the shine of the mirror gone?" "The shine of the mirror" means that if the mirror is completely empty, then it is just brightly shining. Our mind, like a mirror, continuously casts images; thoughts are flowing nonstop. When an image is formed, where has the shine gone? At that time, where is the mind's original radiance?

That is like saying that in meditation my mind may become still, quiet, serene, clear, one-pointed, focused; then all of a sudden images, images, thinking, thinking, feeling, feeling, all these things appear. Where has original quiet gone? Where has original brightness gone at the moment thinking begins to appear and form?

After the Zen master asked his question, various people came forward, presenting different answers. But he did not like any of them. Then a monk came forward, bowed, and said, "Still not far off."

"Still not far off"—that is called Zen faith. Even at the moment of image after image appearing, still not far off. Intimately close, in fact. Closer than is imaginable. So image after image, form after form, that is called miraculous display. No problem. At that time: Original radiance is still not far off.

But the cigarette man does not understand this. So he clings to oneness, without seeing oneness in diversity. He makes a lopsided oneness, then attaches to it. He loses his ability to function and respond to circumstances appropriately.

Zen Master Seung Sahn sometimes likes to teach the cognitive aspect of Zen understanding by using loosely organized schemas. At one time he would use a circle and point to the different degrees on the circle as indicating different facets or aspects of Zen mind. Now, of course, in a circle 0 degrees and 360 degrees are the same point, which means that where you start from and where you complete the circle are not different points. This is a representation of "Zen mind is beginner's mind"; there is no before and after; no coming and no going. Most radically, this means this moment in its completeness. Seung Sahn would also always be careful to warn students that ultimately the circle and its degrees do not exist. It is only a teaching device that was not to be attached to or reified. To use a teaching schema or device is certainly not new in the Zen tradition. During the Tang dynasty in China (618–907 CE), schema were used by various teaching lines. In the Soto tradition there were five ranks that described five different ways of viewing the relationship between the absolute and the relative and between the real and the apparent. The Lin-chi (Jap., Rinzai) tradition also had its formulas. There were classifications of host and guest, the host being that which never moves and the guest being something that comes and goes. Lin-chi would also talk about the four different functions of his famous Zen shout, "KATZ!"

Another form of presentation of Zen Master Seung Sahn's teaching describes three points, which are clearly stated: substance, truth, and function: "First, we teach substance by using one action, such as holding up a finger, shouting KATZ!, or just hitting the floor. Next, we teach about *truth world*: the cushion is yellow, the floor is brown, the wall is white, the sky is blue. There is nothing that is not truth. Everything is truth, everything is clear. If we can attain this truth world, then we can use it in our function—to help suffering beings everywhere. We call this function the *bodhisattva way*."[5] The "Dropping Ashes on the Buddha" kong-an is a way of testing the student's attainment and assimilation of these various facets of Zen mind.

In the doctrinal and sutra traditions there is a similar schema called the *four wisdoms*. The first is the wisdom of great equality (being able to see that all things share the same basic principal or substance or essence). The second is the great mirror wisdom, seeing things as they are (mountains are mountains, rivers are rivers). The third is the great discernment wisdom, or perceiving the exact characteristics of all things. One could say that discernment wisdom is a refinement of the mirror wisdom; one perceives that the mountains are high and that rivers are flowing. The last is the perfecting of action, or using the perception of equality and the exact characteristics of all things, people, and situations to help this world, in compassionate, selfless action.

Not long ago I received a newsletter from the Providence Zen Center containing an interchange between Zen Master Seung Sahn and a student. The student said, "This world is continuously changing. So how come there is only one correct answer to a kong-an?"

Dae Soen Sa Nim replied, "This world is constantly changing? I did not know that. I thought this world was completely empty."[6]

The point is that if you see this world as changing, changing, changing, that is your perspective. Someone else says, "No, no, this world is not just changing, changing, changing. This world is completely empty. Form is emptiness." But a third person says, "No, this world is not completely empty, this world is truth." That means, if your mind is completely empty, like a bright, shining mirror, then each and every thing is reflected therein. Its true nature and true being appear in the mirror. "Sky is blue" appears, "tree is green" appears, "floor is brown" appears. Each is just expressing the truth of its particular being and nature.

Or think about the ocean, an image used frequently in Buddhist philosophy. First, perceive the essential nature of water. Then, consider that this ocean is giving rise to wave after wave, each with its own unique character, form, and qualities at any given moment—and each an expression of the power of the entire, essential ocean.

Yet, also observe that each particular wave is in relationship with many others. So from that perspective, there is nothing but relationship. This wave is interdependent with that wave. That wave is interdependent with this wave. Likewise, I am talking, so you are listening. You are listening, so I am talking. So that is about relationship; there is nothing but relationship. If there is nothing but relationship, then what is our correct relationship with each and every thing, moment by moment?

Someone says, "This world is not empty world, this world is truth world." Another person says, "No this is not just truth world, it is great love, great compassion, bodhisattva-function world." That means, if your mind is clear, if you perceive the depth and then reflect clearly, perceiving each thing just as it is and honoring each thing for its own unique expressiveness, then what is your relationship to this, that, and the other? How do you use yourself in this world? Are you self-centered? Or not self-centered? How? That is where function and relationship appear.

Now, back to the guy with the cigarette and the ashes: He only understands that everything is all one. When he drops ashes on the Buddha, that is like saying, "Buddha, ashes, everything is all just one." Like pea soup. You cook up all the peas until they loose their distinctness and become just puree. The man with the cigarette has become attached to that perspective. He does not perceive that each thing simultaneously maintains its distinctness and its own characteristics; he also fails to perceive his own relationship to all these things.

So how can we help him fix his mind? How can we fix our own, so we perceive all of these together and realize that everything is unified in some way, that we are all somehow of the same family? And that even though this is true—that we are all of the same family, and all one—there are still distinct characteristics that must be respected and honored and appreciated. If we do that, that is true freedom.

There is also the notion that the attachment of the bodhisattva—the vow to save all beings—is actually freedom. The bodhisattva's *saving* has a particular kind of meaning. In that sense, to *save* something is to see its value and to take care of it. Taking care of something is a very different kind of attachment. Entering into a life of caring and of being cared for is not the same as clinging tightly to something out of fear of letting go— fear that then the whole thing may fall apart and I may die, or God knows what will happen.

Remember Dok Sahn's *"mu,"* or *nothing*? There's not much to hold onto there. Yet Dok Sahn walked into the dharma room still carrying his bundle—his *mu* bundle—and exclaimed quite loudly, *"Mu."* So the commentator wrote, "Completely exposed."

Holding momentarily is not a problem; it is rigidity that becomes the problem. If you clutch to something as if the whole of existence depends on it, then nothing comes of it.

A student once said to me, "I've recently come to New York from Kansas and am having culture shock. There are so many people here who seem to need things, to need help, and I don't know how to help them. Sometimes it seems that it may be better not to help them."

I said, "Yes, not helping may actually be helping them in some instances."

The student responded, "I feel really confused in my practice and in knowing how to help people. Am I holding onto ideas I brought to New York from Kansas?"

I replied, "Kansas is quite distinct from New York, so you left the kong-an of Kansas and entered the kong-an of New York. Different kinds of kong-ans hit different areas of your mind. The New York kong-an is a complicated, complex one, with no easy solution. With some kong-ans, you have an intuitive flash, 'Oh yes, simple!' The New York kong-an is not quite like that. One can spend several lifetimes working on the kong-an of New

York City. Don't be too despondent after a few days of being here. It is disorienting at first. From one perspective, the kong-an of New York is something that you may never pass or solve. But whatever you do with sincerity—in any particular day, any particular moment—is an expression of your compassion. When you see so much suffering and don't know what to do, or feel a certain sense of remorse coming from your heart, that is the expression of your enlightened activity at that moment. Sometimes, out of that, something else will become clear: Perhaps a feeling of something to do, or something not to do. And sometimes you will just be confused. I hope you enjoy your stay in New York. I think you will learn a lot here."

Here is a short story about Zen Master Soeng Hyang (Barbara Rhodes) that speaks to this point of not holding rigidity, and about functioning in a helping way. Several years ago, Zen Master Soeng Hyang (actually, this happened before she became a Zen master) wrote an article describing her work as a hospice nurse.[7] She told about making a home visit one day to a woman who was dying of cancer and suffering a tremendous amount of pain. She had worked with this woman and her family for some time, and had introduced visualization exercises and sitting in silence. The family was Roman Catholic, so sometimes they would try a silent prayer. On this day, she gave the patient a shot of morphine to ease the pain, then said to the woman and family members, "Let's sit silently and pray for ten or fifteen minutes." When they looked at each other again, the patient smiled warmly at Soeng Hyang. Apparently the morphine, along with the meditation, had worked. Soeng Hyang recalled thinking, "Yes, this is how it's going to be." The woman would have this wonderful home death, and her smile reminded Soeng Hyang of Mahakashyapa's smile when Buddha held up his flower. How satisfying it was to be this wonderful hospice nurse, providing this wonderful home death.

But then the woman's condition changed, and Soeng Hyang worried, "That's not how it is supposed to be. What happened?" That thought arose over and over again as the woman's disease and her own adaptability took unusual turns. It was not "this smooth, wonderful home death that I, this wonderful hospice nurse, give to you." In reporting this process, Soeng Hyang genuinely reveals the way that she, at that time, would get stuck, then have to reflect back on herself and find some way of letting go while opening to the next experience. In a death and dying situation, the course of events and the flow of life will rip you open at times, almost as if there is no choice but to go with it.

At the end of the story, the woman passes away and Soeng Hyang joins the family after the funeral. They had their Catholic ideas and prayers, she said, and she had her Buddhist ideas and practices. But no one, she wrote, knew where this woman had gone. Catholics could not adequately tell where she had gone; neither could she, a Buddhist. No one really knew. All they knew was that during her final days, this woman's process had been a great teaching to all of them.[8]

Don't hold anything.

NOTES

INTRODUCTION

1. Seung Sahn. *The Whole Is a Single Flower*. Ed. by Jane McLaughlin and Paul Muenzen. Rutland, VT: Tuttle, 1992, p. 47.
2. Ibid., 49–50.

MA-TSU'S FOUR WORDS AND ONE HUNDRED NEGATIONS

1. *The Blue Cliff Record*. Trans. by Zen Master Seung Sahn. Cumberland, RI: Kwan Um School of Zen, 1994, p. 88.
2. Hsing-Hsui. "I thought it was Houbai (the thief) but here is even Houhei (who robbed by trickery)." Quoted in *The Book of Serenity*. Trans. by Thomas Cleary. Boston: Shambhala. 1998, p. 25.

MEDITATION IN ACTION

1. *A Buddha from Korea: The Teachings of T'aego*. Trans. by J. C. Cleary. Boston: Shambhala, 1988, p. 101. Reprinted by permission of the publisher.
2. Ibid., 102.
3. Ibid., 103.

4. Ibid., 107.

5. Ibid., 108.

6. Ibid., 106.

7. Ibid., 109.

8. Ibid., 110.

9. Ibid., 130.

10. Brother David Steindl-Rast. *Gratefulness, the Heart of Prayer*. Ramsey, NJ: Paulist Press, 1984, p. 179.

THE WORLD AS SPIRITUAL PRACTICE

1. *A Buddha from Korea: The Teachings of T'aego*. Trans. by J. C. Cleary. Boston: Shambhala, 1988, p. 145.

2. Ibid., 149.

3. Ibid., 146.

4. Ibid., 147.

5. Ibid., 145.

6. Ibid., 149.

7. Seung Sahn. *Bone of Space*. Cumberland, RI: Primary Point Press, 1992, p. 11.

8. Shunryu Suzuki. *Zen Mind, Beginner's Mind*. Ed. by Trudy Dixon. New York: Weatherhill, 1973, p. 62.

9. *Providence Zen Center Newsletter*, v. 8, no. 4 (1996): 2.

MIND REVOLUTION

1. *A Buddha from Korea: The Teachings of T'aego*. Trans. by J. C. Cleary. Boston: Shambhala, 1988, p. 162.

2. *The Mu Mun Kwan*. Trans. by Seung Sahn. Cumberland, RI: Kwan Um School of Zen, 1984, p. 31.

THE TEACHINGS OF KYONG HO

1. Mu Soeng. *Thousand Peaks: Korean Zen – Tradition and Teachers*. Cumberland, RI: Primary Point Press, 1991, p. 169. (Adapted with permission from Kyung-bo Seo, *A Study of Korean Zen Buddhism Approached through the Chodangjip*, 1969, and reprinted with permission from Primary Point Press).

2. Ibid., 166.

3. *Providence Zen Center Newsletter*, v. 9, no. 2 (1977): 2.

OUT OF THE NET

1. Seung Sahn. *The Whole World Is a Single Flower.* Ed. by Jane McLaughlin and Paul Muenzen. Rutland, VT: Tuttle, 1992, p. 11.
2. Ibid., 107.
3. Seung Sahn. *The Compass of Zen.* Ed. by Hyon Gak Sunim. Boston: Shambhala, 1997, p. 319.
4. Cheng Chin Bhikshu. *Manifestation of the Tathagata: Buddhahood According to the Avatamsaka Sutra.* Boston: Wisdom Publications, 1993, p. 9.
5. Kabat-Zinn, Jon, *Wherever You Go, There You Are: Mindfulness in Everyday Life.* New York: Hyperion, 1995.

ZEN MASTER KO BONG'S "DIAMOND PARAMITA"

1. *Providence Zen Center Newsletter,* v. 5, no. 2 (1993): 1.
2. John Blofeld. *The Zen Teaching of Instantaneous Awakening by Hui Hai.* Totnes, Devon, U.K.: Buddhist Publishing Group, 1987.
3. *Providence Zen Center Newsletter,* v. 7 no. 2 (1994): 1.
4. Seung Sahn. *Chanting and Temple Rules.* Cumberland, RI: Kwan Um School of Zen, 1991, p. 51.
5. *Providence Zen Center Newsletter,* v. 7, no. 8 (1995): 1.
6. *Providence Zen Center Newsletter,* v. 7, no. 2 (1994): 1.
7. *Providence Zen Center Newsletter,* v. 8, no. 3 (1996): 1.
8. *Providence Zen Center Newsletter,* v. 7, no. 2 (1994): 1.
9. *Providence Zen Center Newsletter,* v. 7, no. 2 (1994): 1.
10. Shunryu Suzuki. *Zen Mind, Beginner's Mind.* Ed. by Trudy Dixon. New York: Weatherhill, 1973, p. 66.
11. Ibid., 66.
12. *Providence Zen Center Newsletter,* v. 7, no. 2 (1994): 2.
13. *Providence Zen Center Newsletter,* v. 7, no. 2 (1994): 4.

ZEN MASTER SEUNG SAHN'S
"DROPPING ASHES ON THE BUDDHA"

1. Seung Sahn. *Bone of Space.* Cumberland, RI: Primary Point Press, 1992, p. 57.
2. Seung Sahn. *Dropping Ashes on the Buddha.* Ed. by Stephen Mitchell. New York: Grove Press, 1976, p. 85.

3. *The Blue Cliff Record*. Trans. by Zen Master Seung Sahn. Cumberland, RI: Kwan Um School of Zen, 1994, p. 21.

4. Ibid., 15.

5. *Primary Point* 5, no. 1 (1988): 1.

6. *Primary Point* 14, no. 2 (1996): 1.

7. *Primary Point* 5, no. 1 (1988): 3.

8. *Primary Point* 5, no. 1 (1988): 3.

GLOSSARY

Aitken, Robert, b. 1911. From 1959 until his recent retirement, roshi of the Diamond Sangha in Honolulu, Hawaii, which he founded with his wife Anne Hopkins Aitken.

Amitabha (Jap. Amida). A buddha honored by the followers of Pure Land Buddhism.Usually translated as Buddha of Infinite Light, or Infinite Time, Infinite Space.

Ang Sahn (Chin. Yang-shan; Jap. Kyozan), 807–890. Chinese Zen master and student of Zen Master Wi Sahn (Chin. Kuei-shan). Together their teaching became the Wi Ang School of Zen, the first of the five major teaching streams of Chinese Zen. Their teaching emphasized the unity of substance and function.

bodhi. Literally "awakened" or full of insight.

Bodhi tree. The fig tree at Bodh-gaya in India under which Siddhartha Gautama was sitting when he attained enlightenment.

Bodhidharma (Chin. P'u-t'i-ta-mo; Jap. Daruma), ca. 470–ca. 543. The twenty-eighth Indian patriarch after Shakyamuni Buddha; the First Patriarch of Zen. He reputedly came to China in 520 and sat for nine years facing a wall at Shao-lin Monastery. His teaching style was quite radical, and introduced the experience of direct mind-to-mind transmission, not depending on words or concepts.

Bodhisattva. An earthly or transcendent enlightened being ready to help others. One whose practice is aimed at the enlightenment of all beings rather than just the enlightenment of oneself.

Buddha Hall. The room in a monastery where monastics and visitors revere the example of the Buddha by bowing and chanting.

Buddha nature. The Mahayana Buddhist ascribes this term to his or her true self. According to Zen all things have Buddha nature and the innate potential to become Buddha. From the most radical viewpoint, all beings are already Buddhas but they have not yet awakened to the experience of this.

Ching-shan. Zen master and monk of the Niu-T'on School of Zen who lived at the time of the great master Ma-tsu (709–788). He is also called Tao-chin and Fa-chin.

Chinul, Pojo, 1158–1210. Celebrated Korean Zen master who contended that an initial awakening has to be supported simultaneously with the cultivation of *samadhi* (concentration) and *prajna* (wisdom). He is known for his practice maxim "sudden enlightenment, gradual cultivation."

Chogye International Zen Center of New York. One of 85 branches and 21 prison groups of the Kwan Um School of Zen founded by Zen Master Seung Sahn. www.cizny.org.

Dae Mai. Student of Ma-tsu. His name means "Great Plum" in Korean and Chinese. When his practice had matured, Ma-tsu said, "The plum is ripe."

dana-paramita. The perfection of giving.

Dharma. The teachings of the Buddha. Also translated as "truth" and "phenomena," the meaning being that all phenomena are continually teaching the Buddha's truth.

dhyana-paramita. The perfection of meditation.

"Diamond Paramita." Zen Master Ko Bong's teaching on the essence of the six *paramitas* as practiced in Mahayana Buddhism and Zen.

Dogen Zenji (1200–1253). Introduced Soto Zen to Japan. One of the most revered Zen masters in the Japanese tradition. He traveled to China in 1223 and there experienced a profound enlightenment. He returned to Japan in 1227 and taught extensively. The sincerity of his practice is greatly admired, as is the profundity of his writings.

Dok-Sahn (Chin. Te-shan; Jap. Tokusan) ca. 781–ca. 867. Initially a sutra scholar from Szechuan, who later became an acclaimed Zen master. A famous kong-an tells of his visit to Zen Master Wi Sahn.

don't-know mind. Mind before thinking. Sometimes also referred to as "great doubt." Ultimately, the clear perception and functioning of the original mind, unhindered by conceptual thinking and imposed ideas of good and bad. That which can connect appropriately with the situation at hand moment by moment.

Five Precepts. The traditional Buddhist guides for conduct. They are: (1) I vow to abstain from taking life, (2) I vow to abstain from taking things not given, (3) I vow to abstain from misconduct done in lust, (4) I vow to abstain from lying, and (5) I vow to abstain from intoxicants, taken to induce heedlessness.

Four Great Vows. The central intentions of the Mahayana bodhisattva path. They are: (1) Sentient beings are numberless; we vow to save them all; (2) Delusions are endless; we vow to cut through them all; (3) The teachings are infinite; we vow to learn them all; and (4) The Buddha way is inconceivable; we vow to attain it.

"Great Dharani of the Mystic Mind Energy." A long mantra associated with the Bodhisattva of Universal Compassion.

Hae Bong. Korean Zen master who asked Ko Bong, "How many pounds does your mind weigh?" One of the major Zen masters of the modern Korean Zen period.

Hae Jae. Means "loose Dharma" in Korean, as contrasted with *Kyol Che,* or "tight Dharma." *Hae Jae* marks the end of *Kyol Che,* the traditional ninety-day group retreat. At the end of the retreat there is a closing ceremony and dharma talk by the Zen master, then *Hae Jae* begins and lasts for the next three months, until the beginning of the next *Kyol Che.*

Hong-jik. Korean Zen master, a student of Hsi-tsang. One of the first Korean monks to go to China and bring Zen back to Korea. Started one of the Nine Mountains Schools of Zen in Korea.

Hsi-tsang (Jap. Seido), 734–814. Successor of Mat-tsu. Great Chinese Zen master who trained several Korean monks before they brought Zen back to Korea.

Hua-yen Sutra (San. *Avatamsaka Sutra*). A long Buddhist scripture that teaches the interconnectedness and mutual identity of all phenomena in the cosmos. Through vast cosmic imagery it teaches the interpenetration of the one and the many; that one particle of dust contains the entire universe, and that one moment is identical to infinite lengths of time.

Hui-k'o (Jap. Eka) 487–593. The Second Patriarch, dharma successor of Bodhidharma. He is said to have cut off his arm as a sign of his deep sincerity and longing for the teaching.

Hui-neng (Jap. E'no) 638–713. The Sixth Patriarch; considered to be the author of the *Platform Sutra*. From his successors emerged the five main teaching streams of Zen in China during the Tang dynasty.

Hwagyesa. Temple founded by Zen Master Shin-wol in 1522 in the foothills of Mount Sam Gak, northeast of Seoul. Zen Master Seung Sahn established the International Zen Center for overseas students within the temple grounds in 1984.

hwadu. Essential point in a kong-an story used as a topic of meditation. Literally means "wordhead" or "head of speech" in that it points to the original mind from which words and ideas flow.

Hyech'oi. Student of Zen Master Hsi-tang before his death in 814. Started one of the Nine Mountains Schools of Zen upon his return to Korea from China.

Ikkyu, 1394–1481. Witty and profound Japanese Zen master. His practice was quite radical and free, not conforming to the orthodox style.

Ji Bong (Robert Moore). Received transmission from Zen Master Seung Sahn in 1997. He is the Guiding Teacher for a number of Zen centers: Dharma Sound (Seattle), Great Brightness (Las Vegas, NV), Dharma Kai (Whittier, CA), Ocean Eyes (Long Beach, CA). He is also a professor of music composition and theory at the University of Southern California.

Joju (Chin. Chao-chou; Jap. Joshu) 778–897. Great Chinese master. His teaching is the quintessence of Zen. His style is sometimes referred to as lips-and-tongue-Zen in that he usually did not resort to drastic methods like shouting at or hitting his students, but used simple words in unusual ways to open the student's mind.

kasa. A brown piece of cloth worn around the neck or over the shoulders of Zen monastics or people who have taken the Five Precepts, symbolic of Buddhist vows and precepts. The *kasa* has several folds that are sewn to form rows. The *kasa* represents the original patchwork robe of Buddhist monks and nuns and is representative of renunciation.

KATZ! Traditional Korean Zen shout used to cut off discriminative thinking.

KoBong, 1890–1961. Zen Master Seung Sahn's teacher who gave him transmission. It was the only transmission Ko Bong ever gave.

kong-an (Korean for *koan*). A paradoxical question or problem given to a Zen student by a Zen master aimed at cutting through conceptual thought. They are used in Zen training as a focusing device, and as a way of helping you to see into the inherent non-meaning of words and to realize the absolute nature of reality.

kshanti-paramita. The perfection of patience, endurance, or perseverance.

Ku Sahn Sunim, 1909–1983. Korean Zen master. One of the most renowned of the modern Korean Zen masters. He started an international Zen meditation center in Korea, where he taught both Westerners and Asians.

Kwan Hwa. The emphasis in Rinzai Zen to perceive the kong-an: illumination through looking into words.

Kwan Seum Bosal. A mantra that in Korean means "one who perceives the cries of the world and responds with compassionate aid." Also the Korean name for the Bodhisattva of Compassion, known variously as Avalokiteshvara (San.), Kuan-yin (Chin.), and Kannon (Jap.).

Kwan Um School of Zen. In Korean "Kwan Um" means "hear the cries of the world." Zen Master Seung Sahn founded the Kwan Um sangha in 1972 to act as a fulcrum for teaching Zen throughout the world. www.kwanumzen.org.

Kyol Che. Korean for "tight dharma." An intensive retreat usually lasting from 21 to 90 days.

Kyong Ho (1848–1912). Zen Master Seung Sahn's great-grand-teacher. The main reviver of the Korean Zen tradition in modern times. He is three generations before Seung Sahn in the same lineage.

Layman Pang (ca. 740—ca. 808). Student of Zen Masters Shih-t'ou and Ma-tsu. Great Zen master who continued to live as a layperson after receiving transmission rather than become a monk.

Lin-chi, d. 866/67. Founder of the Lin-chi (Jap. Rinzai) School.

Maezumi Roshi, 1931–1995. Japanese-born Soto Zen master who founded the Zen Center of Los Angeles (1967) among other centers.

Magoksa Temple. Temple in S. Korea founded in 642 on the south side of Mount Tachwasan. High above this temple, Zen Master Seung Sahn did his first one hundred day retreat in a small hermitage on the mountain.

Mahakashyapa. One of the Buddha's first disciples. When the Buddha held up a flower in front of twelve hundred monks assembled at Vulture Peak, only Mahakashyapa smiled. With this understanding smile he became the Buddha's successor.

Man Gong, 1872–1946. Zen Master Seung Sahn's grandteacher. Considered one of the greatest of modern day Korean Zen masters. In Seung Sahn's lineage, he is two generations earlier.

mandala. Usually a colorful series of concentric circles in which buddhas, bodhisattvas, gods, and demons are represented. Mandalas are used in ritual and visualization practices in Tantric forms such as Tibetan Vajrayana and Japanese Shingon Buddhism.

mantra. Sounds or words used in meditation to cut through discriminating thoughts so that the mind can become clear.

Ma-tsu (Jap. Baso Doitsu; Kor. Ma Jo), 709–788. One of the great Chinese Zen masters. He was the first to use radical methods such as shouts or hitting the student to bring about a sudden awakening of insight.

Mind-Only School. Uses the phrase, "the revolution of consciousness" to describe the sudden transmutation of the deep unconscious (storehouse consciousness) into an experience of awakening to the true mind. Teaches that to realize the ultimate truth, one should view the nature of the universe as created by mind alone. This school teaches that we make our own version of reality through mental representation. Furthermore, it attempts to undo dualistic thinking through postulating pure subjectivity or original mind.

mu. Japanese and Korean word meaning no, also nothing! Many Zen students use this word *mu* as the subject of their kong-an practice. It comes from the famous remark of Zen Master Joju: A monk asked Joju, "Does a dog have Buddha nature?" Joju responded, "Mu." The focus of the kong-an is, "What is the meaning of Joju's 'mu?'"

Mu Mun Kwan (Chin. *Wu-men-kuan*; Jap. *Mumonkan*). *The Gateless Barrier*: a collection of kong-ans. This is one of the most used kong-an collections in Zen. Composed by Zen Master Mu Mun (Chin., Wu-men, Jap., Mumon) in the early 1200s. It contains forty-eight kong-ans with a short commentary and poem after each one.

Muk Jo. In Soto Zen this means "to perceive silence"; to just sit and "hit" the world of opposites. That is, to cut through the duality of subject and object, inside versus outside, through just sitting in silent meditation.

Namu Myoho Renge Kyo. Mantra meaning "Veneration to the Sutra of the Lotus of the Good Law." Chant of the Nichiren tradition.

Nan-ch'uan (Jap. Nansen; Kor. Nam Cheom), 748–835. Great Chinese Zen master. Was a main successor of Zen Master Matsu and the teacher of Joju. Taught Korean monks who returned to Korea to start the Nine Mountains Schools of Zen.

Nichiren. School of Japanese Buddhism named for its founder Nichiren, 1222–82. The teaching revolves around the *Lotus Sutra* and the central practice is the chanting of the name of the sutra as a mantra. It is a socially active school that is lay-oriented rather monastic.

Nine Mountains Schools. Earliest Zen tradition in Korea, beginning early ninth century.

Om Mani Padme Hum. Traditional Buddhist mantra meaning "Om, jewel in the lotus." This mantra appears in the *Thousand*

*Hands and Eyes Sutra,*which is chanted daily in Korean temples. The sutra says that this mantra reveals the original mind of the Bodhisattva of Compassion.

paramitas. The six perfections, the central practices of those following the bodhisattva path of Mahayana Buddhism. They are: 1. *Dana* (generosity) 2. *Shila* (morality) 3. *Kshanti* (patience) 4. *Virya* (energy) 5. *Dhyana* (meditation) 6. *Prajna* (wisdom).

Poep An (Chin. Fa-yen; Jap. Hogen), 855–958. Outstanding Chinese Zen master. When asked the meaning of his pilgrimage he replied, "Don't know." He is the founder of the last of the five main teaching streams or houses of Zen in China during the Tang dynasty.

prajna-paramita. The perfection of wisdom.

Pure Land. Usually refers to the "Western Paradise" where one may be reborn before entering nirvana. In the Pure Land School there is constant recitation of the name of Amitabha.

qigong. Manifestation of internal force or energy. Usually relates to certain breathing and visualization practices in Chinese Taoism and Buddhism.

Rinzai School (Chin. Lin-chi-tsung). See Lin-chi.

sangha. The community of all practitioners as well as individual groups.

San-sheng (Jap. Sansho; Kor. Sam Seong). Ninth century successor to Lin-chi. He is mentioned in several kong-ans in *The Blue Cliff Record,* including a case called "The Golden Fish Who Has Come through the Net."

Satchidananda, Swami, 1914–2002. Founder of Integral Yoga and a disciple of Swami Sivananda. Integral Yoga brings together the practices of the main streams of yoga, i.e., Raja, Hatha, Bhakti, Karma, and Jnana yoga, seeing them as complimentary rather than contradictory.

Seol Bong (Chin. Hsueh-feng; Jap. Seppo), 822–908. Influential Chinese Zen master. From his teaching line two of the five Zen schools of Chinses Zen arose, the Un Mun (Chin. Yun-men) and Poep An (Chin. Fa-yen).

Seung Sahn, b. 1927. Born in N. Korea. Dae Soen Sa Nim (Korean for Great Honored Zen Master), as he is known by the sangha of the Kwan Um School of Zen, came to the US in 1972, where he established the Kwan Um sangha.

Shakyamuni Buddha, b. ca. 563 BCE Siddhartha Gautama of the Shakya clan, the historical Buddha.

Shao-lin Monastery. Founded in 497 in the Songshan Mountains of China, site of Bodhidharma's nine-year retreat facing a blank cave wall in 527.

Shariputra. One of the Buddha's foremost students. Shariputra appears in several of the sutras, including the *Heart Sutra* and the *Vimalakirti Sutra.* He is sometimes used in the Mahayana sutras to represent the limitations of the Hinayana approach.

Shi Shim Ma. Korean for "What is this?," Emphasized by Chogye Zen in perceiving don't-know mind.

Shingon. Japanese Tantric school of Buddhism. It is the only remaining school of what was originally the Chinese Tantric tradition. Its practices use mantras and visualization of mandalas, as well as ritual gestures (*mudras*).

Shunryu Suzuki Roshi, 1904–1971. Japanese-born Soto Zen master who founded the San Francisco Zen Center and established

Tassajara, the first Zen monastery in the West. Author of *Zen Mind, Beginner's Mind*.

Sivananda, Swami, 1887–1963. Founded Divine Life Society in 1936. Modern Himalayan Yogi who promoted a popular resurgence of interest in yoga throughout India.

Soeng Hyang (Barbara Rhodes). The Vice Zen Master and Guiding Dharma Teacher of the Kwan Um School of Zen, and the Guiding Teacher of Zen centers and groups in Connecticut, Florida, Chicago, and Colorado. She received transmission from Zen Master Seung Sahn in 1992. A registered nurse since 1962, she works for Hospice Care of Rhode Island.

Sosan Taesa, 1520–1604. Korean Zen master, author of *Handbook for Zen Students*. He was a major revitalizer of Korean Zen during his lifetime. His *Handbook* is still widely used in Korean Zen.

Soto School (Chin. Ts'ao-tung-tsung). Japanese school in which sitting is emphasized as opposed to the Rinzai sect where koan practice is considered the main approach.

Su Bong, 1943–1994. American Zen master who received dharma transmission from Zen Master Seung Sahn in 1992. Died in Hong Kong where he was the Guiding Teacher of the monastery now named for him.

Sudoksa Temple. Korean temple near Yesan founded in 599 or perhaps earlier. The Main Hall was built in 1308; its architecture is considered to be the oldest and most pleasing wooden structure in the country.

sutra. Discourses of the Buddha, used for study and the practice of recitation. The literal meaning of sutra is "thread." Sutras contain the main threads of the various Buddhist teachings and philosophies.

Tachu. Successor of Zen Master Ma-tsu; wrote *Discourse on the Essential Teachings of Entering the Way Through Sudden Awakening.*

T'aego, 1301–1382. Korean Zen master who was responsible for consolidating the Nine Schools into the single school of Chogye.

Tantric. Often associated with esoteric practice. Uses mantra, visualization, and ritual gestures called *mudras* in some of its practices.

Toui, d. 825. Korean Zen master who visited China in 784, studied under Hsi-tang. Returned to Korea in 818.

true nature. That which cannot be grasped through ideas or concepts and is therefore before thinking.

Un Mun (Chin. Yun-men; Jap. Ummon), 864–949. Eminent Chinese Zen master. Founder of one of the five main teaching schools of Chinese Zen, Un Mun is famous for his one word or short phrase answers. A monk once asked Un Mun, "What is Buddha?" Un Mun said, "Dry shit on a stick."

Vairochana. Great universal Buddha of Light. The central Buddha of the *Avatamsaka Sutra.* He is considered to be a personification of the absolute or dharmakaya body of the Buddha.

virya-paramita. The perfection of energy.

Wi Sahn (Chin. Kuei-shan; Jap. Isan), 771–853. Renowned Zen master visited by Dok Sahn. Founder, along with student Ang Sahn (C., Yang-shan) of the first of the five Chinese Zen schools. His teaching used the terms "substance" and "function" to represent the unmanifest and the phenomenal.

Won Hyo, 617–686. Revered by all Korean Buddhists for the inclusiveness of his teaching. He synthesized the various teachings of the Mahayana sutras and philosophies in a harmonious way so that the apparent contradictions were resolved. He also encouraged the common people to practice chanting the Buddha's name. Won Hyo was both a monk and a layperson at different times in his teaching career.